STO

**ACPL ITEM
DISCARDED**

S0-BKX-404

AUG 27 '65

Foundations of Modern Economics Series

Otto Eckstein, *Editor*

AMERICAN INDUSTRY:
STRUCTURE, CONDUCT, PERFORMANCE
Richard Caves

PRICE THEORY
Robert Dorfman

MONEY AND CREDIT: IMPACT AND CONTROL
James S. Duesenberry

LABOR ECONOMICS
John T. Dunlop

PUBLIC FINANCE
Otto Eckstein

ECONOMIC DEVELOPMENT: PAST AND PRESENT
Richard T. Gill

ECONOMIC SYSTEMS
Gregory Grossman

INTERNATIONAL ECONOMICS
Peter B. Kenen

NATIONAL INCOME ANALYSIS
Charles L. Schultze

PRENTICE-HALL, INC., ENGLEWOOD CLIFFS, NEW JERSEY

FOUNDATIONS OF MODERN ECONOMICS SERIES

Otto Eckstein

Harvard University

PUBLIC FINANCE

PRENTICE-HALL
FOUNDATIONS OF MODERN ECONOMICS SERIES

Otto Eckstein, *Editor*

© *Copyright 1964 by PRENTICE-HALL, INC., Englewood Cliffs, New Jersey.*

All rights reserved. No part of this book may be reproduced

in any form, by mimeograph or any other means, without permission

in writing from the publishers. Printed in the United States of America.

Library of Congress Catalog Card No. 64-13088.

Designed by Harry Rinehart

C-73750 (p), C-73751 (c)

PRENTICE-HALL INTERNATIONAL, INC., *London*
PRENTICE-HALL OF AUSTRALIA, PTY. LTD., *Sydney*
PRENTICE-HALL OF CANADA, LTD., *Toronto*
PRENTICE-HALL FRANCE, S. A. R. L., *Paris*
PRENTICE-HALL OF INDIA, PVT. LTD., *New Delhi*
PRENTICE-HALL OF JAPAN, INC., *Tokyo*
PRENTICE-HALL DE MEXICO, S. A., *Mexico City*

1309928

FOUNDATIONS
OF MODERN ECONOMICS SERIES

Economics has grown so rapidly in recent years that no one book can present it authoritatively today. *Foundations of Modern Economics* is a series of concise books surveying the major branches of the discipline, each written by a leading economist in the midst of the research and discussion of his specialty. Taken individually, each book reflects the structure, the content and the key scientific and policy issues of its field. The Series as a whole presents an account of Economics designed to be the material for the basic one-year college course.

v

Two of the nine books present the analytical core of Economics, *Price Theory* and *National Income Analysis.* Study of one or both of the core books is recommended before entering into the various fields of application. *Economic Development: Past and Present,* which uses a more historical approach, can be read without prerequisite and can serve as an introduction.

This new approach, as compared to the usual textbook, has several advantages. By mirroring the actual state of knowledge and discussion, the books gain in interest, depth, and relevance. They also communicate some of the excitement of the current research in a developing field.

The books free the teacher to devise his own course curriculum, rather than to follow the format of the textbook. Any selection or order of topics is possible once analytical principles have been mastered. Specific areas can be explored at greater length. The teacher not interested in a complete survey course can eliminate several of the books, spending more time on detailed study of a few fields. One-semester courses, emphasizing only micro-economics, or only macro-economics, can also be readily devised.

The books do not offer settled conclusions. They show the student the central problems of each field, and show how economic analysis permits more intelligent thinking about them. The Series is offered in the hope that this firsthand exposure will equip the student better as a citizen, and will attract him to the further pursuit of the subject.

Otto Eckstein, *Editor*

CONTENTS

Introduction, 1

1

The Scope of Government Activity, 3

How Big is Government in the American Economy? *Purposes of Government Expenditures.* *Reasons for Growth of Government. Are There Laws of Growth of Government Spending?* *Defining the Proper Scope of Government Activity.* *Controversial Border Areas between the Private and Public Sectors.* *The Ballot Box versus the Market Place.* *Summary.*

2

Efficiency in Government Expenditures, 20

Budgeting. *Budget Concepts.* *Efficiency Devices.* *Concluding Notes: The Political Reality.* *Summary.*

3

The Public Finances of State and Local Governments, 33

The Advantages of Local Government. *Advantages of National Programs.* *Post-War Financing of State and Local Governments. State Tax Systems.* *Solutions to the Problems of State and Local Finance.* *Summary.*

4

Economics of Metropolitan Areas, 43

Trouble in the Core City. Problems in the Suburbs. Problems of Coordination and Planning: Physical Interdependence Ignored. Metropolitan Consolidation? Alternatives to Metropolitan Consolidation. Summary.

5

Taxation: Principles and Issues of Fairness, 51

Some Basic Concepts. Some Practical Criteria for Tax Systems. A Fair Tax System: Criteria of Equity. Measures of Ability to Pay: The Choice of Tax Base. Vertical Equity: The Structure of Tax Rates. The Federal Personal Income Tax. Issues of Fairness. The Double Taxation Issue. Summary.

6

Taxes, Efficiency, and Growth, 70

The Tax System and the Efficiency of the Economy. Progressive Income Taxes and the Supply of Effort. The Tax System and Economic Growth. The Tax System and Personal Saving. Too Much Income Taxation? The Search for Alternatives. The Tax System and the Growth of Demand. Concluding Comments. Summary.

7

Budget Policy for Economic Stability, 84

The Theory of Fiscal Policy. The Budget Principles of Fiscal Theory. Deficits and Surpluses: Automatic and Discretionary Changes. The Full Employment Budget. Some Complications. Other Budget Principles: The Annually Balanced Budget. Budget-Balancing at Full Employment; The CED Plan. Actual Fiscal Policy against Recession. Actual Fiscal Policy during Inflation. Suggestions on Improving Fiscal Policy. Summary.

8

The Economics of the Public Debt, 105

Growth of Debt. The Structure of the Debt and Debt Management Policy. A Policy Dilemma. Recent Improvements in Debt Management Technique. Summary.

Selected Readings, 116; Index, 117

INTRODUCTION

Government is big and important in our economic system. The American people rely on government to protect individual freedom, to maintain social justice, to furnish a variety of public services, and to provide a system of laws which permits the functioning of a free market economy based on private property. The economic quality of government goes a long way to determine the performance of the entire economy. If government is inefficient, resources are wasted and tax burdens are unnecessarily high. If government does too much, private performance deteriorates: Individual households and businesses are no longer able to exercise their initiative effectively and to reach the rational, decentralized decisions which are essential for a properly functioning market economy. If government does too little, private economic power may be exercised in ways detrimental to the economy as a whole; disparities in income and wealth may become too great; and public services may be provided in a manner unworthy of a great and wealthy country.

This book is an introduction to public finance, the study of the revenue and expenditure activities of government. It deals with budgets, with taxes, with government expenditures, and with public debts. These are only a few of the many aspects of the economics of government. The book does not deal with government regulation of industry, the government's role in labor-management relations, the proper management of the money and credit system, or with our economic relations with the rest of the world.

Public finance is the study of the effects of budgets on the economy, particularly the effect on the achievement of the major economic objectives—growth, stability, equity, and efficiency. It is also the study of "what ought to be": Assuming that we wish to accomplish certain objectives such as increased growth or a fairer distribution of income, what specific policies will accomplish the objectives?

An understanding of public finance should help you grapple meaningfully with such key public issues as:

1. How wide should the scope of public activity be?
2. What is the proper level at which a public service should be performed—federal, state, or local?
3. Is our tax system threatening the growth of the economy?
4. Why have state and local governments fallen on such hard financial times? And how can they be helped without placing all control in Washington?
5. How can government best combat the business cycle, given the inevitable human failings of delay and occasional misjudgment?
6. Why should we be worried about the national debt?

This book will not settle these questions for you. You will have to add your own philosophical values, your view of human nature, and even a little of your own emotions—how you feel about government—to reach your own conclusions. But economics is a large part of the story, and you cannot make much sense of these questions without it.*

* I am grateful to Harvey Brazer, Martin David, and Richard T. Gill for helpful comments on the entire manuscript, to Samuel M. Cohn on Chapters 1 and 2, and to Joseph A. Pechman on Chapters 5 and 6. I also wish to thank Alfred Goodyear, Wilbur Mangas, and James Murray of Prentice-Hall for their most skillful editorial counsel, and for their great help at every stage of the development of the Foundations of Modern Economics Series.

1

THE SCOPE OF GOVERNMENT ACTIVITY

How Big Is Government in the American Economy?

Our is a capitalist economy. We rely on private enterprise to supply most of our economic wants. Yet government has grown enormously in size and in the variety of its activities, until today the "public sector" constitutes a fifth of our economy—still leaving four-fifths as the "private sector."

Table 1 shows some of the basic facts for a recent year, 1962. Here are some salient items from that table:

1. Total government expenditures were $168 billion. This is equal to 30 per cent of the gross national product of $555 billion. The federal government spent $110 billion. State and local governments spent $59 billion (including $8 billion provided by the federal government as grants-in-aid).

2. Total government expenditures exceeded receipts, producing a deficit of $4 billion.

3. Only some of these expenditures were *exhaustive,* absorbing real resources such as the labor of government employees or goods and services purchased from business. The rest of the expenditures were non-exhaustive or *transfers,* such as the transfer of money to individuals for social-security or unemployment benefits, to businesses as subsidies, or to other governments as grants-in-aid; the payment of interest on government debt is also considered non-exhaustive.

TABLE 1

The Public Sector, 1962 (Billions of dollars)

	Total	Federal	State and Local
Expenditures	168.5	109.8	58.7
Exhaustive	117.0	62.4	54.6
Government employees	54.6	24.0	30.6
Purchases from business	62.4	38.4	24.0
Transfers	51.5	47.4	4.1
to Persons	32.5	26.7	5.8
to State and local governments	7.7	7.7	—
Other (interest, transfers to foreign governments, subsidies and profits of government enterprises (—) indicates profit)	11.3	13.0	−1.7
Receipts	164.4	105.4	59.0
Personal taxes (income, estate, etc.)	57.7	49.0	8.7
Business taxes (sales, profits, property, licenses, etc.)	75.1	36.0	39.1
Payroll taxes (social security, unemployment insurance, etc.)	23.9	20.4	3.5
Transfers from federal government	7.7	—	7.7
Surplus or Deficit	−4.1	−4.4	+.3

Source: National Income and Product Accounts, U.S. Department of Commerce.

4. Exhaustive expenditures totaled $117 billion; thus, government absorbed 21 per cent of all the goods and services of the economy, about equally divided between the federal level and state and local governments. This part of total output is allocated by governmental decisions, not private choices. Transfers, on the other hand, merely shift purchasing power from one decision unit to another, with the recipient determining how the money shall be spent.

5. Not all the exhaustive expenditures are the result of direct government economic activity; half represents government purchases of the products

of private enterprise, such as missiles and school buildings. They represent private production devoted to public uses.

No one numerical magnitude can fully reflect the importance of government in the economy. The level of total taxes is significant: Each dollar of taxation, whether spent on exhaustive expenditures or transfers, represents a little bit of compulsion. It can affect private incentives and the growth of the economy. Total exhaustive expenditures show the share of GNP allocated by government. Total expenditures on government employees show the extent of government production.

Furthermore, some government activities which cost practically nothing are extremely important. The numerous regulatory activities, the administration of justice, and the creation of new laws by the Congress and the president mold the institutional shape of the economy. Certainly their dollar cost is no measure of their significance.

Purposes of Government Expenditures

For what purposes is the money spent? Table 2 shows a breakdown of major government expenditures.

At the federal level, defense, international affairs, and the cost of past wars—interest and veterans' benefits—account for $69 of $122 billion for 1964. The space programs add another $4 billion. The remainder is chiefly for welfare transfers like social security and unemployment insurance, for agriculture and resource programs, for transportation, housing, and the general administrative costs of government.

TABLE 2

Government Expenditures by Function (Billions of dollars)

Federal Expenditures *	1962 Act.	1963 Est.	1964 Est.	State and Local Expenditures †	1962
National defense	51.5	53.4	56.0	Education	21.2
International affairs and finance	2.5	2.5	2.7	Highways	9.2
Space research and technology	1.3	2.4	4.2	Police	2.2
Agriculture and agricultural resources	6.0	6.8	5.8	Fire	1.2
Natural resources	2.2	2.5	2.6		
Commerce and transportation	5.5	6.2	6.7	Prisons	.8
Housing and community development	1.7	.9	1.1	Relief	5.0
Health, labor, and welfare	24.0	25.8	27.4		
Education	1.1	1.3	1.5	Health, water supply, sewers, etc.	6.4
Veterans benefits and services	6.1	6.4	6.0	General government	8.4
Interest	6.9	7.5	7.7		
General government and other	— .9	1.0	.7	All other	4.3
Total expenditures	107.7	116.8	122.5	Total expenditures	58.7

* *Source:* The Budget of the United States Government, 1964. The figures are for the Consolidated Cash Budget, hence differ by a small amount from Table 1. (See Chapter 2 for a discussion of conceptual differences of the two sets of budget figures.)
† *Source:* National Income and Product Accounts, U.S. Department of Commerce.

Education takes much the largest share of state and local government expenditures. The provision of such local services as highways, police and fire protection, water supply and sewers, and a heavy load of relief payments are the other major cost items.

FIG. 1   Growth of government expenditures, 1929-1962.

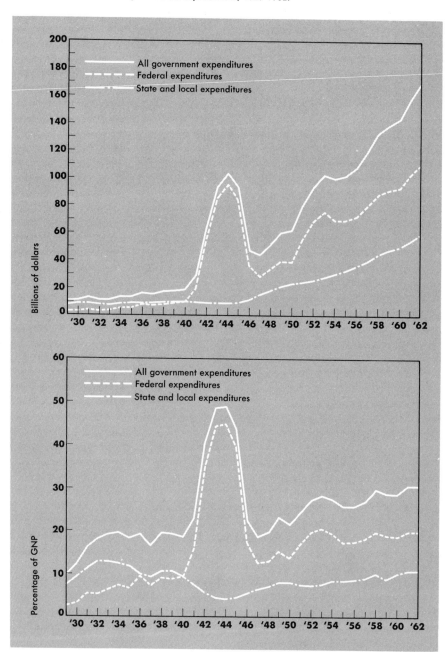

Thus, apart from defense, the federal government is more a reshuffler of money—taxing on the one hand, transferring to individuals and state and local governments on the other—and less a direct manager of civilian activities. The bulk of civilian government services is still provided at the state and local level. But the federal government has tended to preempt the best financing sources, a tale to which we shall return in Chapter 3.

Reasons for Growth of Government

As recently as 1929, the ratio of total expenditures to GNP was only 10 per cent, compared to the current 30 per cent. Why has this increase occurred? Table 3 helps us toward some answers.

1. Defense expenditures are by far the most important reason for the growth of government. In 1939 we spent $1 billion, about 1 per cent of GNP; at the peak of World War II, the figure rose to $89 billion, or 42 per cent of GNP. Through rapid demobilization we cut back to $11 billion 2 years after World War II, only to have to re-arm in a hurry when the Korean War broke out. Since then, defense costs have remained high and have been rising again recently, though their share of the GNP is still considerably less than during the Korean War.

2. The tremendous increase in transfer payments is the second key development. Pensions for the aged, for the disabled and for widows, special programs for veterans, benefits for the unemployed, as well as direct relief payments now apply very widely. With the number of persons over age 65 increasing greatly and the benefit levels improving, these payments have tripled since 1947. The growth of these programs reflects social trends in our society. (a) With urbanization and the resultant breakup of the large multi-generation family household, the retired can no longer count on living with their children and being provided for by them; in a sense, we have socialized the financial support of our aged. (b) Since the 1930's and the New Deal, we have become much more conscious of our obligation to provide minimum incomes for people who have suffered some economic disaster, such as unemployment, disability, or loss of the family wage-earner. It is the adoption and growth of these programs which are sometimes referred to as the rise of the welfare state.

3. The big increase in non-defense exhaustive expenditures has been at the state and local, not the federal, level in the post-war period, chiefly because of the great increase in the number of children who have to be educated in local school systems, and the capital costs for roads, sewers, and the like, for suburbia.

4. At all levels of government, rising prices have been important in recent years. Salaries of teachers, policemen, and other employees have been rising rapidly after having lost ground through the post-war inflations. Productivity in government has risen more slowly than in industry, partly because there is less scope for automation in government, and the pressure normally exerted by the profit motive and competition in industry is missing. Rising salaries in the face of low productivity gains have raised the costs per unit of service. This is just one example of the general cost rise of services. In the case of medical services or haircuts, prices have risen steeply, much more than average consumer prices. In the case of education or other government services, expenditures—and hence local taxes—have gone up.

TABLE 3

Growth of Government Expenditures

	1929	1939	1944	1947	1953	1960	1962
In billions of dollars:							
All expenditures	$ 10.2	$ 17.5	$103.1	$ 43.9	$102.5	$137.2	$168.5
All exhaustive	8.5	13.3	96.5	28.4	82.8	100.1	117.0
Federal	1.3	5.2	89.0	15.7	58.0	52.9	62.4
Defense	n.a.	1.3	88.6	11.4	49.3	45.5	53.3
Non-defense	n.a.	3.9	.4	4.3	8.7	7.4	9.1
State and local	7.2	8.1	7.5	12.7	24.9	47.2	54.6
All transfers to persons	.9	2.5	3.1	11.1	12.9	28.8	32.5
Other transfers (interest, etc.)	.8	1.7	3.5	4.4	6.8	8.3	19.0
As a percentage of GNP:							
All expenditures	9.8%	19.2%	48.8%	18.7%	28.1%	27.2%	30.4%
All exhaustive	8.1	14.6	45.7	12.1	22.7	19.8	21.1
Federal	1.2	5.7	42.1	6.7	15.9	10.5	11.2
Defense	n.a.	1.4	41.9	4.8	13.5	9.0	9.6
Non-defense	n.a.	4.3	.2	1.9	2.4	1.5	1.6
State and Local	6.9	8.9	3.6	5.4	6.8	9.3	9.9
All transfers to persons	.9	2.8	1.5	4.7	3.5	5.7	5.9
Other transfers	.8	1.8	1.6	1.9	1.9	1.7	3.4

Source: National Income and Product Accounts, U.S. Department of Commerce.

5. The scope of government has been increased, a trend that is reflected particularly in the rise of federal purchases of goods and services for civil purposes. This extension of the public sector occurred largely during the New Deal, when new programs in agriculture, housing, and resource development were set up. The transfer programs also were introduced then. Since the New Deal, the scope of government in the domestic economy has been little changed.

Are There Laws of Growth of Government Spending?

The German economist Adolph Wagner, writing in 1883, thought he had discovered the "Law of Ever-Increasing State Activity" upon surveying the public-expenditure records of several advanced countries in the nineteenth century. He based his "Law" on the "pressure for social progress and resulting changes in the relative spheres of private and public economy, especially compulsory public economy." History has certainly borne him out, though war and its aftermath have cost more than social progress.

Recently, Peacock and Wiseman at the London School of Economics have tested Wagner's ideas with modern statistics for Britain.[1] They found his "Law" still working, but they provide a rather more complicated expla-

[1] Alan T. Peacock and Jack Wiseman, *The Growth of Public Expenditure in the United Kingdom* (National Bureau of Economic Research, 1961).

nation. They find that expenditures grow because revenues grow, rather than the other way about: A given tax system with constant tax rates yields more money as the economy grows, and governments, like most of us, somehow spend their income. Furthermore, the cost of providing public services grows with the nation. There is usually a substantial gap between people's notions about desirable expenditure levels when they think of the benefits, and the amounts they accept as tolerable burdens of taxation. The

FIG. 2 Total government expenditure and GNP, United Kingdom, at current prices, 1890-1955. (*Source:* Peacock and Wiseman, *op. cit.*, p. 43.)

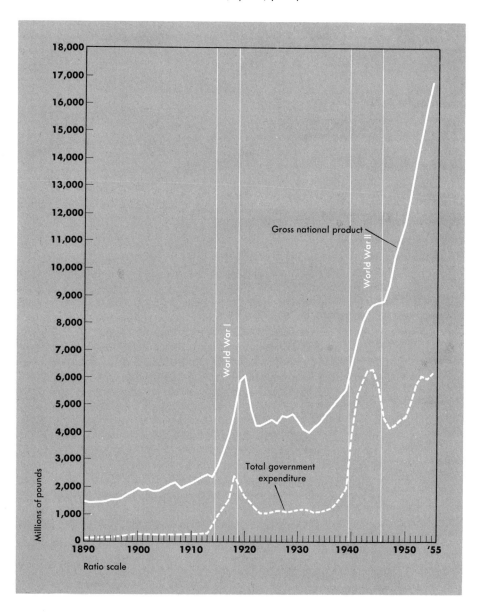

pressures for larger budgets from beneficiaries and the bureaucracies of operating agencies are always immense. To the extent that revenues are available, the guardians of the public purse (the budget bureaus and treasuries of the world) have little power to refuse requests. Only when action is required to raise tax rates to finance the new spending can they say "No!" and make it stick.

Besides this gradual growth of expenditures in line with revenues, every few decades the necessity to finance a war leads to a widening of the tax system. Once the war is over, the system does not return to its pre-war level; some of the new taxes and higher rates are continued, so that the growth trend of revenues and expenditures is moved upward permanently (see Fig. 2). This movement is called the "displacement effect." Wars also have led to a general re-examination of government's responsibilities, and have been followed by the adoption of new social-welfare programs.

The theory seems to fit fairly well for British experience. Does it also apply to the United States? At best in a rather general way. Tax rates at the federal level do not change very frequently, and aside from wars, expenditures have moved pretty much in line with revenues. The displacement effect has occurred, especially after Korea, but can largely be explained by the continued need for high military expenditures.[2] Furthermore, except for veterans benefits, wars have not produced social legislation; the New Deal was a result of depression, not of war. If there is a will, expenditures can even be reduced while revenues grow, as President Eisenhower showed in the late 1950's. Thus, while there inevitably is a lot of momentum in existing spending programs and a growing country needs more public services, long-term movements in expenditure levels are as much the result of conscious policy decisions by the president and the Congress and by ourselves, the voters.

Defining the Proper Scope of Government Activity

What is the proper scope of government? Are there economic criteria which can help us to decide whether an activity should properly be in the public or in the private sector? This question has concerned thinkers from ancient times. Adam Smith, founder of classical economics, confined the list to (1) defense, (2) the administration of justice, and (3) certain public works.[3] Today, three approaches to this question can be discerned: (1) Permit government action only when the private market cannot do the job; (2) Permit a more active role for government; (3) The socialist approach.

PERMIT GOVERNMENT ACTION
ONLY WHEN THE PRIVATE MARKET CANNOT DO THE JOB

Private enterprise, operating in a market economy, will meet most desires of consumers in an advanced country like ours. There are, however, some limited situations in which the market cannot function properly; then government takes some action. These situations have certain economic characteristics which cause the market mechanism to fail:

[2] State and local governments, on the other hand, which have not had the benefit of the displacement effect, have been forced to adopt new taxes and to raise rates steadily in the last 15 years as their costs have risen.

[3] Adam Smith, *The Wealth of Nations* (New York: The Modern Library, 1937), introduction to Book V.

1. *Collective goods.* These are goods and services that have certain characteristics that make it altogether impossible to provide them through the market. They have two related qualities: First, they inevitably have to be supplied to a group of people rather than on an individual basis. Second, they cannot be withheld from individuals that refuse to pay for them.

Take national defense, for example. The national security provided by our military forces is extended to all persons in the country. They all receive the same degree of protection, whether they are willing to pay for it or not. There is no way of withholding the service, of creating a market which separates those who pay from the freeloaders. In fact, in this type of situation, the rational, wholly self-interested consumer of economic theory will never pay since he will get the benefit in any event.[4]

In the case of ordinary private goods, this difficulty does not occur. If one person likes some item of food or clothing or a service, and another does not, one will pay for it and receive it, the other will not. If someone should refuse to pay yet wish to obtain the product, the sellers would simply refuse to give it to him. This crucial distinction has been called the *exclusion principle:* A good is *private* if someone who does not pay can be excluded from its use. If it cannot be withheld (violating the exclusion principle), it is a *collective* good.

Defense is not the only collective good. Other expenditures for foreign-policy objectives—foreign aid, space exploration, and so on—exhibit the same quality. Some domestic cases are flood control, where a dam protects all the persons in a valley whether each agrees to pay or not, police and fire protection, and the administration of justice. (The examples tend to match Adam Smith's list.)

Not all goods supplied jointly to many people are collective goods. In some instances the exclusion principle applies. The services of a movie theater can be enjoyed by many people at about the same cost as by one; but the service is marketable since admission can be denied to those who refuse to pay. Roads and parks are on the borderline; sometimes they can be withheld, sometimes not.

2. *Divergencies between private and social costs or benefits.* In order for private decisions based on market prices to lead to the economically best result, prices must be sound indicators of social benefits and costs. In a well-working competitive market economy, prices reflect the relative values of different goods to consumers, as well as the marginal costs of producers, thus equating marginal values to consumers with the marginal costs of producers. Prices serve as a signaling device of benefits and costs. But in some situations, a private decision-maker may not have to pay for all the costs he causes the economy; in others he may not be able to reap all the benefits. The prices he will be using in his decisions will not fully measure the true values to the economy as a whole; consequently, prices will cease to yield correct signals and private decisions based on them will not produce an optimal result. These divergencies are sometimes called *external economies* or *diseconomies.*

For example, a paper mill which pollutes a river imposes a cost on society for which the mill is not charged. It reduces the value of the river to the economy, yet the mill will not consider this cost in its profit-maximizing

---

[4] But notice that it is rational for him to *cast his vote* for defense expenditures plus the taxes to finance them. For then he will not have to pay unless everyone else is also compelled to pay through taxation.

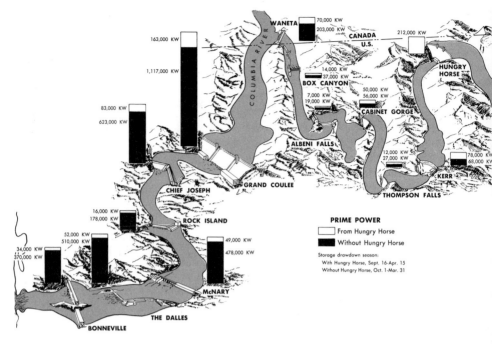

FIG. 3 Downstream benefits for power production of the Hungry Horse project. (*Source:* J. V. Krutilla and O. Eckstein, *Multiple Purpose River Development* (Baltimore: Johns Hopkins Press, 1958, p. 63. Adapted from chart published by Bonneville Power Administration.)

calculations. Conversely, when Western Electric scientists invented the transistor, other companies, both in the U.S. and abroad, gained far more than any patent royalties they may have paid, not to mention the benefits to consumers and the Defense Department!

Usually these unrecompensed benefits and costs are minor and do not constitute sufficient cause for government intervention, much less government operation. No one would argue that just because one corporation puts up an eyesore of a skyscraper while a more tasteful company beautifies the city with its headquarters, the one company should be penalized or the other rewarded. But sometimes the divergencies between the private and the public benefit-cost calculus become so great that the activity must fall within the scope of government. Here are two cases:

Figure 3 shows the economics of a typical storage reservoir in the West, at Hungry Horse Dam, which carries over water from wet seasons to dry and also from wet years to dry. When the water is released, it passes through 12 downstream dams, generating power at each one—in fact, three-fourths of the resultant power is developed at the downstream dams. A private company would not develop Hungry Horse; most of the benefit would accrue to other private power companies, some local public companies, and the U.S. government. The result: Hungry Horse is a public-power dam.

But while government intervention was necessary, public ownership was not the only possible solution. A private company might have been given the legal power to collect a fee for the benefits it was providing to others; the federal government might have paid a private company a subsidy to compensate for the downstream benefits; a voluntary association of down-

12

**FORT WAYNE
NATIONAL**
that's my **BANK**

stream beneficiaries might have been formed to put up the money for the dam; or a mixed private-public setup could have been devised under which the federal government might have built the dam, and left the power equipment to be provided by private enterprise. But in our society we do not like to pay subsidies to large companies, or to give private companies what amounts to the power to tax. And voluntary associations are not easy to organize when conflicting interests are involved. So situations of this sort often lead to government operation.

A more important but less clear-cut example is education. Everybody gains from living in a democracy with an educated citizenry. Also, some of the economic benefit of having an educated labor force accrues to employers through lower production costs, and to consumers through lower prices, though it is impossible to determine precise amounts. Here too there is a choice of method of intervention. Schools could be public, or parents could be given subsidies to pay tuition in private schools. In this case, we have chosen public operation, partly because it is more efficient, but mostly for non-economic reasons.

3. *Very heavy risks.* While American private enterprise thrives on risk-taking, some types of risk can be undertaken only by government. For example, private companies could not develop atomic energy as a source of electric power. The total research cost is enormous; a number of years must pass before costs can be brought down to economical levels; and even if one of our corporate giants were willing to take the huge risk, it would find it difficult to reap the benefit by obtaining a patent monopoly and keeping it long enough to recoup its investment. Thus, heavy technological risk is compounded because the benefits cannot be fully appropriated by the risk-taker. Two forms of intervention have been used in such situations: direct government activity (e.g., government laboratories such as Los Alamos and Huntsville), or more commonly, government contracts to private industry (as in the development of giant computers, supersonic airliners, and most space work).

4. *Natural monopolies.* The supply of electricity, gas, telephone service, and mass transportation usually is carried out most effectively if one organization alone provides the service in a community. Average costs fall with size, and if two or more companies compete, they may have to provide wasteful duplicate facilities. Thus, a monopoly is typically the most efficient supplier. But without competition to set limits on profits, some form of public intervention is necessary to assure reasonable prices. In most countries, the state operates such enterprises directly; in the U.S., government operation is not the typical pattern, though it is found in some regions. Instead, public agencies regulate price and service standards, but leave ownership and management in private hands.

5. *Other reasons.* This list does not exhaust the theoretical bases for government activity, even where there is a general presumption in favor of doing things privately. The government has responsibility for general economic policy to *prevent depression and inflation,* matters discussed elsewhere in this book. The use of the *power of eminent domain,* under which the government can force people to give up land and to move, say, to permit a highway to be built or for slum clearance, may lead to government activity, since we do not favor entrusting this power to private persons. Sometimes government activity is just a question of *convenience* and *low cost;* for instance, weather forecasting could be a private enterprise and some of it is. But it is

handy to have one central data-collecting agency, and also to have it issue some forecasts; it costs very little, and supplies the information to everybody.

Many Americans take a different philosophical position. Rather than limit government to situations in which the private market fails, they see government in three additional roles: (1) as a competing source of initiative; (2) as changing the pattern of private consumption; and (3) as a means of redistributing income.

1. *Government as a source of initiative.* Initiative and innovation can appear anywhere in a society. Managers in the public sector may see an opportunity to provide some service in a new or better way, just as in the private sector. Most government programs are quite far removed from commercial undertakings, and hence initiative is not likely to be applied competitively with private enterprises. But there are exceptions. The issue then arises whether the public agency that introduced the innovation should be allowed to develop it.

The Tennessee Valley Authority, which produces electric power (besides providing navigation, flood control, and other services) is an example of government initiative. In its heyday, the TVA had exceptional foresight in realizing the potential of a high-volume, low-cost market for power; it also had the most efficient steam power plants in the world.[5]

Why? In the 1930's when TVA was organized, the private-power industry was handicapped by the low profits and the negative psychology of the depression; the TVA, a famous social experiment, attracted some of the finest young talent available. After years of prosperity, private companies have the means of matching—and in a few cases surpassing—TVA's technical efficiency, and the huge size of the market for electricity at low rates is now appreciated by everybody.

In America, with its many centers of private initiative, such examples of successful government enterprise are rare and usually associated with depression.[6] In contrast, in some underdeveloped countries, where the number of potential entrepreneurs is very small, one can expect government to play a sizable innovating role, even in industry.

2. *Changing the pattern of consumption.* In some situations, government rejects the decisions of consumers in the market economy and substitutes its own judgment. This is atypical in America (apart from discouraging the use of drugs, liquor, and tobacco through regulation and high taxes), but there are cases where government acts to increase the supply and lower the cost of some good or service, or even compels its consumption. Housing is the most substantial instance. The federal government has numerous programs in this field: public housing projects for low-income families, urban renewal grants for slum clearance, mortgage guarantees, a tax system which gives preferential treatment to home ownership.

[5] TVA also had the advantage of very favorable tax treatment and of having access to low-interest public capital, as its critics justly charge. But this does not explain away its genuine achievements.

[6] The mortgage insurance program of the Federal Housing Administration is another example. Started in 1934 as an anti-depression measure, this program has been earning over $100 million a year in premiums, building up a large insurance reserve. But who could have the foresight at the bottom of the depression to see that the loss rate on insured mortgages would be almost negligible while the insurance premium which people eagerly paid was ½ per cent?

Insurance against certain economic hazards is another consumer service prescribed through the political process. Social security is, after all, a compulsory pension scheme to insure against poverty in old age. Unemployment insurance is another example.

3. *Redistributing income.* Some government activities are intended to redistribute income. Besides transfer payments, some public works are built and some lines of production subsidized (e.g., agriculture) to raise the income of a particular group. The U.S. Congress has authorized a $1 billion project to make part of the Arkansas River navigable. It is hard to justify this project in terms of the commercial benefit to be gained by the country from the boat traffic that can be expected. But the project is in a poor region with little prospect of improvement without government help. Building the waterway will raise the income in the area, the construction activity itself generates some local income, and the navigable river will improve the marketing of crops in the area and may attract industry. It might be cheaper to pay cash subsidies instead of authorizing a huge construction project, but subsidies would be politically unacceptable.

THE SOCIALIST APPROACH

Farther to the left on the political spectrum (off scale in the U.S. but not everywhere else) is the socialist approach to the scope of government: If other things are roughly equal, let an activity be public rather than private. If one accepts Marx' doctrine that the private ownership of the means of production leads to the inevitable exploitation of the workers, then industry should be owned by the workers acting through their government, and any private ownership of capital becomes suspect. The most doctrinaire socialist would admit that government cannot run everything efficiently, that some things must be left to private enterprise. Even in Russia, a tiny private sector of petty merchants and handicrafts survives, and farmers on collectives are allowed small plots of their own to cultivate; and in Yugoslavia, a less doctrinaire country, the state enterprises have some of the characteristics of private enterprises, with much independent decision-making by the firms' managers, some price determination in markets, and with wages and salaries tied to enterprise profits.

The problems of public finance in socialist countries differ in some important respects from those in a free-enterprise economy. With industry state-owned, the government must determine the economy's price and production policies. Production decisions are made through a central plan which sets the production targets for industries and their plants. Price policies become an important instrument of public finance. By allowing itself high mark-ups on costs, the government can raise funds to finance its activities, including new investments. On the whole, socialist countries have not used their tax systems to promote income equality as much as we have. They defend their attitude on the grounds that with capital publicly owned, the income distribution produced by the economic system is satisfactory. This book will not take up the socialist approach in any detail, since our interest is primarily in public finance in the United States, and the socialization of industry is a dead issue here.[7] But keep in mind that not all peoples share our philosophical point of departure that every government activity requires some special justification.

---

[7] Another book in this Series, *Economic Systems,* by Gregory Grossman, deals with the socialist approach.

Even outside the communist countries, socialism is still a widely held idealistic goal. Particularly in underdeveloped countries such as India, it is capitalism which is on trial, and activities are likely to be conducted privately only if private operation can be shown to be superior.

Controversial Border Areas between the Private and Public Sectors

On the whole, the American people pretty much agree on the proper scope of government. We want ordinary productive activities privately owned and run, and private goods allocated through markets. We also agree that government must provide collective goods and other goods which are not suitable for market processes.

Our differences are not about capitalism versus socialism as economic systems but about certain areas of the economy. These have been persistent bones of contention between private companies and public agencies competing in the arena of public opinion for the privilege of developing them, or at least of halting the inroads of the other. In terms of the economy as a whole, the areas under dispute are small; in terms of newspaper space, immense. Here are the key cases:

Electric power. The federal government started out in this business when it produced power as a by-product of dams built for flood control and navigation. Later, it built pure power dams if they were part of a river basin program that was designed to accomplish the other objectives. And in the Tennessee Valley, after the private systems had been bought out and the river had been fully developed, the TVA built steam-electric plants, a precedent the private-power companies considered ominous. At its peak in 1958, federal public power accounted for 17 per cent of all power sold in this country; by 1960 the figure had dropped to 15 per cent.[8] For a while it appeared that the old battles would be refought over atomic energy, but for a long time it was not a sufficiently attractive commercial proposition to make it worth fighting over, and now it is viewed as just one more form of power equipment.

Insurance. Issues keep cropping up in this area. In the 1930's social security was considered a government invasion of the private insurance field. In the early 1960's medical insurance for the aged had become the point of controversy. Private companies argued that voluntary private plans would cover most retired people within a decade anyway. Advocates of compulsory public insurance contended that medical costs of the aged had become very high, too high for their low income, making illness another economic disaster against which the government ought to provide security.

Commercial activities of the Defense Department. Some fringe activities of the military establishment have been under fire as undue invasions of private enterprise. Military post exchanges have been criticized for gradually becoming small department stores, underselling local merchants while enjoying immunity from some sales taxes and possibly making the taxpayer bear part of the overhead costs. A lot of posts have had government-run laundries, when commercial laundry service could have met the need. During the 1950's the government closed several thousand such small enterprises in a program to end commercial-type government activities.

[8] But local public-power systems, especially in the Northwest, continued to increase their share of the market, keeping the total public share almost level at 24 per cent.

The Military Air Transport Service (MATS) maintains our capability to move troops quickly to trouble spots. It also uses its planes to provide transportation for military personnel and their dependents. In the spirit of American enterprise, MATS kept on improving its product, making flights more regular, replacing bucket seats with comfortable interiors, and adding stewardesses and meals. Private airlines objected to the subsidized competition, and succeeded in keeping MATS from obtaining congressional appropriations to buy jet transports. When it became foolish not to have our emergency transport capability on a jet basis, a compromise was worked out in which MATS got its new planes, but reduced its direct competition with the airlines, leaving to them more of the routine transport services.

Communications satellites. A clear indication of our preference for regulated capitalism over public ownership can be seen in the recent controversy about the management of the coming worldwide communications satellite system. The development of the rockets required to launch the satellites is inevitably a public undertaking. On the other hand, civil radio communication has traditionally been a private industry. The obvious policy alternatives were to (1) have the federal government build and operate the system, or (2) assign the task to the American Telephone and Telegraph Company, which would be the biggest user, and which has the research know-how. These solutions proved unattractive; government operation would be a public invasion of a new industry; A. T. and T. participation would strengthen its monopoly position in international communications. Instead, a new kind of institution was invented, a private corporation partly owned by the major communication companies, partly by the general public, with exceptionally stringent government regulations, particularly about matters of international political sensitivity. This is still an experimental approach.

Other cases. Here are two other examples. One, lumber companies disagree with the Forest Service about the management of our national forests. Should they be left strictly for future use, or should some of them be made available for commercial development? Two, what should be government's role in providing the vast, needed expansion for outdoor recreation facilities? Should there be more national parks, reservations, and similar public facilities, or should we rely primarily on private enterprise?

To resolve such questions, more than economics is involved. Economic analysis may show how close to our notion of a collective good a specific activity comes, or how significant divergencies between the private and the social benefits and costs may be. But these considerations have to be weighed against the costs of the concentration of power in the hands of government, and the imperfections of public operation.

The Ballot Box versus the Market Place

Decisions in government and in the private economy are reached quite differently. Supply and demand in markets determine spending and production decisions in the private sector. In the public sector these decisions are made through the political process. Viewed as decision-making machinery, the major differences are these:

Government decisions involve an element of compulsion. An individual in an ordinary market is free to purchase or not purchase, but once the government has decided to supply some service, all individuals are compelled to share in paying for it through taxation. In the case of collective goods, this is inevitable. Since they cannot be withheld, they cannot be financed through voluntary market decisions. Therefore, if a majority of individuals (or rather their elected representatives) feels that a collective good is worth its cost to the community, it will vote to have the government provide it and to tax everyone to pay for it. An individual affirmative vote on an expenditure and a tax is not a decision to actually spend money; the spending and taxing will occur only if the majority approves, compelling everyone to share the cost. Thus, some people pay for services they do not want—even pacifists have to pay taxes for defense. While this may be the only effective way of financing genuine collective goods, the same principle of compulsion applies to other kinds of public expenditures. Thus, all taxpayers contribute to the financing of agriculture, veterans' benefits, housing, and numerous other programs even though many people may have no desire for them.[9]

Without the test of the market, there can be no assurance that a public service will actually render benefits greater than its cost. In the private sector, if a good does not provide satisfaction in excess of its cost, the company producing it will suffer losses; but governments collect their taxes even if a specific good that they supply proves unsatisfactory.

The political process is an insensitive choice mechanism. Government provides many services. But the voters can be expected to assess only a very small number of issues in any one election. Thus, the voter has to register his preference about a package of issues, whereas in the market place he can decide about each good separately.

Decisions made by the political process reflect the distribution of political power among pressure groups, regions, and the like. This influences the pattern of government expenditures. The groups that are well-organized receive more benefits than the rest, and succeed in redistributing income from the unorganized to themselves. What's more, hardly any expenditure program, regardless of its importance to the country as a whole, is unaffected by the power distribution. The location of space research facilities, the closing of defense installations, and other such decisions are influenced at least in a minor way by political strength. The pattern of distribution of public-works spending is more heavily determined by politics than by more rational criteria.

These considerations make the political process look inferior to the market mechanism. But there are some points on the other side.

In the market place, dollars are votes; in the political process, each person has one vote. A society in which all the voting was done by dollars would be inequitable. In a sense, the political process represents a safety valve for our capitalist system, through which we modify the income distribution generated by it. This is clearly seen in such programs as public assistance and unemployment insurance, which aid individuals for whom the economic system is yielding particularly low incomes. But it is also illustrated by housing and agricultural programs, in which we reject the results of dollar voting in favor of spending decisions registered through the political process. With a different distribution of voting rights, the political process will produce a result different from that produced by the market. And after all, ours is a democracy of people, not of dollars.

---

[9] Not all expenditures are financed this way. A few, such as power projects, produce revenues sufficient to pay their cost. Others, such as most highways, are paid for out of earmarked taxes levied on the users.

In some situations, the market system cannot operate effectively. For true collective goods there is no alternative to collective action, and these include such important matters as the defense of our liberty. Even where goods are marketable, divergencies between private and social benefits and costs or the presence of monopoly power may cause markets to produce imperfect results.

The relevant comparison is not between perfect markets and imperfect governments, nor between faulty markets and all-knowing, rational, benevolent governments, but between inevitably imperfect institutions. The general recognition of the imperfection of all the alternatives may account for the decline of doctrinaire socialism or of doctrinaire laissez faire-ism in the United States. Perhaps it also accounts for the stability in the division between the private and public sectors in our economy that we have reached in the last decade.

Summary

Government plays a large role in the economy, as regulator of the private sector, as supplier of public services, and in many other ways. Public Finance is the study of government's taxing and spending activities.

Government absorbs one-fifth of the total output of the nation's goods and services. It also redistributes large amounts of income through a system of transfer payments to households, to businesses, and from one level of government to another. Government expenditures have been rising, both absolutely and relative to total output. In recent years, the greatest growth has been at the state and local levels.

The definition of the proper scope of government activities can be partly based on such theoretical concepts as collective goods, differences in private and social benefits and costs, and natural monopolies. But these must be combined with philosophical values about the relative desirability of public and private action. The United States has generally favored private over public action, but not all countries share our preference in this matter.

Decisions in the private sector are made through the market mechanism, in the public sector through the political process. Each of these processes has its own advantages and imperfections. The market is free of compulsion and permits more sensitive expression of individual preferences. But its votes are based on dollars, and individuals are not equals in their possession of these voting rights. The political process is based on individual votes. The redistributions of income that the government carries out are a safety valve of our capitalist system.

The frontier between the private and the public sectors has been stabilized in the last two decades, after some extension of the public sector under the New Deal. There is a wide consensus in the U.S. today to support the present line. A few fields remain in dispute and are subject to much controversy, but these represent a very small share of economic activity.

2

EFFICIENCY
IN GOVERNMENT EXPENDITURES

A fifth of the nation's output is allocated, not by individual choices in markets, but by public decision-making. Can economic principles be derived to guide these decisions so that resource allocation in the public sector will be efficient—i.e., so that the resources are employed to accomplish the public objectives effectively and without waste? In this chapter we study two problems: (1) How are decisions actually made in the public sector? and, (2) How can technical economic analysis contribute to the process?

Budgeting

While it is the general political process which determines government expenditures, it is through budgeting that the specific decisions are reached. A budget is a detailed statement of a government's expected expenditures and revenues, usually for a year.[1] The executive branch of government reaches its expenditure and tax decisions in the preparation of this document; the legislative branch considers the proposals and votes the fiscal plans of the government into law.

The federal budget covers a fiscal year, running from July 1 to the following June 30. But the decision-making process starts more than a year earlier, when agencies prepare their preliminary program proposals with price tags. These are reviewed, after which the president sets down guidelines, indicating the approximate funds to be made available or general principles to be applied in the major fields. Detailed budget requests are then made by the agencies in the fall, and from October to December, the president, working with his elite Bureau of the Budget, reviews and pares down the agency requests, which typically total more than the amount which he wishes to spend. By weighing the urgency of the programs against the fiscal needs of the economy as a whole, he decides on an over-all spending policy. He has to decide whether to balance the budget or to run a surplus or a deficit, and then to bring agency requests into line with his over-all fiscal goals.

Early in January, the president sends his budget to Congress. In a growing number of cases, the spending proposals are first considered by the oversight committees concerned with each program, such as the Foreign Relations and Military Affairs Committees, and then reviewed by the houses of Congress. When new legislation is needed, the oversight committee must act before funds can be voted. They vote *authorizations* for programs and specify policies governing them. But this is only the first stage; the Appropriation Committees and the House and Senate still have to vote the *appropriations* of money, and frequently less is appropriated than is authorized because the Appropriation Committees are usually stingier with the public's money than the committees devoted to specific programs. From January until summer, the Congress acts on the requests, attempting to finish its legislation before the next fiscal year begins. Congress raises some expenditures and refuses (or reduces) some requests; changes are usually small. It takes a stronger position about taxes, where the House Ways and Means Committee usually alters Treasury proposals drastically or even rejects them altogether.

The appropriations give the president the right to make contracts and to spend the money, and usually, but not always, after some further passage of time, the appropriation leads to an *expenditure*—that is, to the actual disbursal of money. In some of the largest fields, including defense and space, the delay between appropriation and expenditure is so long and the backlogs of unexpended appropriations so large that the Congress feels it has lost control over the expenditures.[2]

[1] The budgets of some states and localities cover 2 years.

[2] In exceptional cases, Congress authorizes expenditures directly, skipping the appropriation stage. This may take the form of authorizing agencies to respend the proceeds of loans, or even to commit new funds. This is what is meant by "backdoor financing," because the tough appropriations committees are bypassed.

While the period of decision-making appears very long for a fast-moving world, actually the plans can be and are changed all along the way. Many key decisions by the president are postponed to the last possible moment in December. If economic or international conditions change during the spring, he can change his requests. Congress also watches developments as it acts on the budget and reacts to them. Even during the fiscal year itself, the president can decide not to spend all the money voted, or to go back to Congress for supplementary appropriations.

Before 1920 the United States had no integrated budget at all. Appropriations requests of individual agencies were considered strictly piecemeal, and if a congressman, a newspaper reporter, or just a plain voter wished to discover the government's total spending plans, he would have found it virtually impossible to do so. With government very much smaller then, there was less need for a comprehensive over-all view and for weighing expenditure requests against one another. The heavy expenditures during World War I which produced a deficit much larger than planned, plainly indicated the need for a budget. President Taft had advocated the use of a budget earlier, but the Congress refused to approve its adoption.

We have come a long way since then. Today the budget is a very informative document, showing how each department and its agencies spend their money. To find out what the federal government does, take a look at *The Budget of the United States* (Superintendent of Documents, Washington 25, D.C., $1.50). The presentation of the budget by the president to the Congress each January enables the entire nation to take a look at government activities.

The unity of the budget disappears once it reaches the Congress, as separate committees and separate sub-committees of the Appropriation Committees take up different parts. It has repeatedly been recommended that there be a congressional committee to take up the entire budget each year, to bring all expenditures decisions together, and to deal with such general issues of fiscal policy as budget levels and surpluses or deficits. This is a rather utopian proposal. Congress has to be concerned with the detailed decisions. It does not decide to raise or lower the budget as a whole, but works through the specific items. No one committee could deal with all the questions at once. Under the present setup, however, it is important that the congressmen voting on specific expenditure requests have the over-all economic and financial situation in mind. The present budget makes it possible for them to do so.

Budget Concepts

In one respect the budget has fallen into some disrepair. Starting with the social-security program in the late 1930's, some items of expenditures have been left out or taken out of the budget and organized into trust funds. These trust funds are meant to be self-financing, with certain taxes earmarked for this purpose. At first, the trust funds were limited to transfer programs like social security and unemployment insurance, which Congress meant to be kept as separate accounts and financed out of their own payroll taxes. But as presidents struggled unsuccessfully to reduce the total budget, they extended the use of the trust fund device even to some grants-in-aid to states, such as highways, usually earmarking some revenues as well. Today over 20 per cent of total expenditures are not included in the traditional budget, which we call the *Administrative Budget*. If used for economic analysis, a set of budget figures which leaves out such a large part of the total can lead to serious error. Therefore, in recent years, more emphasis has been placed on the *Consolidated Cash Budget*, a comprehensive statement of all payments and receipts by the government to the public. This budget measures the actual intake and outgo of government money, including the trust funds.[3]

One other concept is widely used, the *Budget on National Income and Product Account*. This budget was designed particularly to be a tool of economic analysis. The Cash Budget is just what it says, a measure of cash flows. For analytical purposes, two corrections should be made. First, the economic impact is not always felt at the time of the cash flows, but may come earlier. For example, the tax revenues may be considered withdrawals of private purchasing power before they are actually paid, if the money is set aside when the liability is incurred. Second, not all cash expenditures have the same impact. Some are for purchases of goods and services or income payments, others are just financial transactions. The budget on National Income and Product Account makes some of the necessary corrections. First, taxes are attributed to the period in which the economic impact is felt rather than when they are paid. Corporate profit taxes, for example, are attributed to the period in which the profits are earned, when corporations, using modern accrual accounting methods, enter the tax liability on their books, rather than later when the cash is actually paid. Second, the Income and Product Account Budget omits expenditures which neither absorb resources nor add to incomes directly, such as the purchases of used assets or of purely financial assets such as mortgages. While this omission may be appropriate for some analyses, it causes a loss of comprehensiveness.

Efficiency Devices

Can economic analysis be applied to budget decisions? The remainder of this chapter shows some of the possibilities.

EQUATING MARGINAL BENEFITS AND COSTS

The ideal principle for budget decisions is clear enough. *Push expenditures for each public purpose to that point where the benefit of the last dollar spent is greater than or at least equal to the dollar of cost.* The line *mb* in **Fig. 4** shows how the benefit resulting from additional expenditures on project *A* first rises, then falls as more is spent. Some moderate level of expenditures for, say, highways, yields very great benefit, since this money can be spent on breaking the worst bottlenecks, reducing deaths and injuries, property damage, time spent traveling, gasoline consumption, and wear and tear on car and driver. Greater expenditures may still yield benefits greater than cost, but there is a point where the additional projects undertaken are in more remote, less traveled places, raising road quality beyond the level for which the cost can be justified by the additional benefits. Thus, frequently, there

---

[3] There is one exception. Only the excess of expenditures over receipts of government enterprises is reported. Thus, the Post Office has total expenditures of $5 billion and revenues somewhat less than that, but only the net difference is in the cash budget.

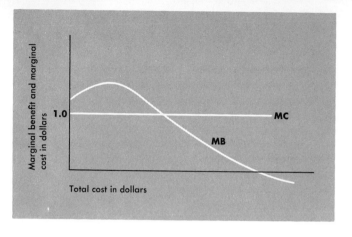

FIG. 4 Equating marginal benefits and costs. Because quantity is measured by dollars spent, the marginal cost curve is just a line parallel to the base, equal to 1.0 (the marginal cost of an extra dollar of spending is a dollar).

comes into play a *law of diminishing benefit*, similar to the laws of diminishing returns and diminishing utility for private goods.[4]

Equating marginal benefits and costs, if it could be done, would solve two problems of resource allocation. It would assure that every expenditure yields a benefit at least equal to the value of goods foregone in the private sector. Second, it would assure that an expenditure does not prevent a more valuable public expenditure in some other field. Thus, the principle assures that benefits of marginal expenditures exceed opportunity costs both in the private and the public sectors.

An example: Design of a Flood Control Project. Flood control is one field of expenditures to which the government applies marginal analyses of benefits and costs. Table 4 summarizes an example. It shows flood damage without protection in a typical year and the lowered damage figures with progressively more ambitious flood protection plans.

[4] But not always! Sometimes, as in curing depressed areas or in urban renewal, only a large-scale effort may succeed. It may be better to pour large sums into a few places rather than spread funds thinly among many.

TABLE 4

Benefit-Cost Analysis of Flood Control for Brink Valley

Plan	Annual Cost of Project	Average Annual Damage	Benefit (Reduction of Damage)
Without protection	0	$38,000	0
Plan A—levees	$ 3,000	32,000	$ 6,000
Plan B—small reservoir	10,000	22,000	16,000
Plan C—medium reservoir	18,000	13,000	25,000
Plan D—large reservoir	30,000	6,000	32,000

Which is the best choice? (Figure out answer before reading further.)

Plan	Marginal Benefit	Marginal Cost
No plan	0	0
Plan A	$ 6,000	$ 3,000
Plan B	10,000	7,000
Plan C	9,000	8,000
Plan D	7,000	12,000

Plan C, the medium-size reservoir, is the best plan. Although it costs $8,000 more than the smaller reservoir, it averts $9,000 worth of damages, so the benefits exceed the costs. A further increment, going to the larger reservoir, would cost an extra $12,000 yet yield only $7,000 of benefits. Thus, this marginal outlay fails the test of having benefits exceed costs—i.e., marginal benefits are less than marginal costs.

The example raises some important points:

1. The principle of equating benefits and costs at the margin can be applied to some expenditures.

2. Real-world data are always subject to error. Actual damages will differ from the projections. The frequency of floods cannot be predicted precisely nor can their damages, particularly for rare but large floods. (Who knows what damage the biggest flood in a thousand years would do? Our history goes back only 350 years, and the early settlers did not spend their time collecting statistics.) Engineering and economic uncertainties must be reckoned with. Construction frequently proves more complicated than expected; prices applied to value benefits may change unpredictably.

3. The definition of benefit assumes that we do not care to whom the benefits or costs accrue—i.e., that income redistribution is not an objective to be pursued through this project. Otherwise it is not enough simply to analyze money values of benefits and costs. Redistributive effects must be measured and judged as well.

4. And most important, it must be possible to define economic benefits measurable in dollars and cents. Even in the field of flood control—a particularly simple one for economic analysis—the definition of benefit is ambiguous. To what extent is lost production made up later on or elsewhere? What is the loss attributable to the feeling of insecurity caused by floods—not to mention that most intractable valuation problem: the worth of a human life?

Can the benefit-cost principle, then, serve to determine the proper allocation of resources for most public expenditures? Unfortunately not, because the dollar yardstick can usually not be adequately applied to the benefits. This is certainly true for the benefit of defense expenditures, of space research, foreign aid, police protection, or the administration of justice. Education, housing, and highways, which are believed to provide considerable monetary benefits, so far have not yielded to reliable measurement. Their benefit is widely diffused and partly non-economic. Could a democracy survive without an educated citizenry? What is the total gain from clearing slums? Thus the benefit-cost principle can be applied only in limited cases like flood control, electric power production, the Post Office, some transportation and recreation facilities—mostly in the public works fields where benefits are primarily economic, tangible, and measurable.

The most important use of the benefit-cost principle may well be negative. It is a useful antidote to two approaches that are widely employed and that are pretty sure to lead to poor results. The first of these is the *requirements approach*. It says that a country "needs" X thousand more new housing units, W million gallons of water, Y dozen nuclear submarines, Z thousand more classrooms by 1970, and that this need is so clear that it must be fulfilled regardless of the cost. In fact, there is always some cost which that "requirement" is not worth. And adding up the "requirements" as seen by the proponents of each program always yields fantastically expensive results. Economic resources are scarce, tough choices have to be made between competing programs, and strong-voiced assertions about requirements and needs do not really help us to reach wise decisions. Benefits must be balanced against costs at the margin.

The other fallacious approach is the "That's what we can afford" or "budget first" approach. It determines the total to be spent before looking at the benefits. While usually employed by opponents of spending who suggest that an extra dollar beyond the arbitrarily set amount would somehow bankrupt the country, the approach also has a spender's variant: "Why are we spending only X per cent of our GNP on (fill in your favorite government service) when we spend Y per cent on liquor and tobacco?"

A firm grasp of the benefit-cost principle will not provide easy answers to expenditure choices. Instead it forces us to pass judgment on the worth of the expenditure at issue, to see if it is worth its tax cost, and whether it represents the best use of the public money. It also focuses the attention of decision-makers on the margins, where the decisions are made. It does not ask: "Is defense worth its cost?" but rather, "Would an extra billion of defense yield an important enough improvement in our strength to be worth the cost?" This is the sort of inescapable question which the president and Congress have to face every year, and which they have to answer even though precise measurement of benefit is impossible.

FINDING LEAST-COST SOLUTIONS

Even though the difficulty of measuring benefits makes a wholly economic approach to expenditure decisions impossible, other more modest and more pragmatic principles of economics can usefully come into play, and have come into extensive use in recent years. One of these is the simple idea of seeking out the least-cost solution of a given problem.

Sound engineering practice has always included this principle, but in such technically complicated fields as defense and space exploration there is usually such a wide range of technically feasible alternative approaches that comprehensive economic analysis is necessary to discover which approach promises to be the most efficient—that is, which will be the one which will accomplish the objective at least cost. For example, what is the most efficient way of maintaining our ability to intervene militarily in East-West skirmishes in Southeast Asia? Is it most efficient to (1) station American troops in many places, complete wth all equipment and supplies; (2) maintain a few central overseas bases plus the means of transporting troops in a hurry to trouble spots; (3) keep the troops in the United States but invest a great deal of money in jet transports to airlift troops and equipment; or (4) put some heavy, bulky, but cheap supplies like gasoline in depots overseas and keep troops and expensive equipment at home for airlift? Only an elaborate analysis would reveal which of these solutions is best. There are many categories of cost to be considered. A decrease in one cost category frequently means an increase in others. If the troops are kept in the U.S., fewer troops are needed and the cost of maintaining bases will be much smaller; but the cost of the required transport capability will climb sharply. Complete overseas bases reduce transport costs but tie up much capital in equipment and require heavy operating and maintenance costs. Intuition or seat-of-the-pants judgment is not likely to produce the correct answer.

In addition, some intangibles also have to be weighed, such as political factors (e.g., the effect of bases on overseas politics), the reliability of the selected method (e.g., immunity from sabotage), its flexibility against various contingencies, and the speed of action. Usually, the decision-maker has to weigh cost differences against these differences in intangibles, and it is at this point that intuition and judgment properly must come into play.[5]

THE PRICING OF PUBLIC SERVICES

For that limited range of public services which are marketable, the government has the choice of providing them free, or of charging for them. The absence of a charge assures maximum use, but it also may lead to waste. Pricing can be used to improve resource use in the public sector.

Pricing is largely a question of economic efficiency. We know from price theory that a market economy requires prices as signaling devices to indicate to producers what value consumers place on their outputs, and conversely, to indicate to consumers what the costs of providing goods and services are to the economy. In the private sector the rule for pricing [6] is this: *Price, in an efficient economy, is equal to the cost of supplying the marginal unit of service, i.e., equal to marginal cost.* In principle, this rule could be carried over to many government services; but in practice, governments frequently underprice their services, sometimes because of the influence of pressure groups, sometimes as a matter of philosophy. Here are a few examples:

The Post Office runs at an annual loss of over half a billion dollars because postal rates are kept low, partly because of public pressure. The result is just what one would expect. Being cheap, the postal service is used wastefully, as the astronomical volume of junk advertising mail attests. This is one of the causes of the deficit. Magazines and books enjoy low rates and add their bit to the losses. In addition, the low rates and the grudging financing of the deficits by Congress have kept the Post Office poor, too poor to be able to finance a proper modernization program. This contrasts with the telephone companies, privately operated enterprises in a similar business, which have a more rational rate structure and which are able to conduct research and take full advantage of technological progress.

The pricing of the use of national parks has been a matter of philosophy. The National Park Service has preferred to keep the parks either free or available at very low charges, to assure maximum use. If one assumes that the marginal cost of additional use of a national park is very low, this policy makes sense. But it is now clear that as use goes up additional facilities have to be provided. Conversely, as the facilities are improved, more people are eager to use the parks. For these reasons the Park Service has raised some of its charges, and has discovered in the process that users do value the parks highly and are generally willing to pay the higher prices cheerfully. It now looks as if higher prices will lead to better parks and greater use.

The pricing of highways is a particularly complicated but important case. Traditionally the U.S. has provided roads without charge, except for tolls on some bridges and some state turnpikes. An obviously inefficient

[5] The RAND Corporation, a non-profit government-financed research organization devoted to military problems, pioneered these methods of analysis. An immense amount of technical information about each alternative together with data about military contingencies are fed into computers and the machines then derive the costs of the systems under various alternative conditions. The Defense Department now applies these techniques to develop the necessary information for its decisions.

[6] See R. Dorfman, *Price Theory,* another book in this Series.

allocation of resources has resulted from this policy. This is seen most clearly in the case of congested city streets. No charge is made at the time of use. As taxpayers, the motorists pay for the city streets, but their tax bill is not related to the frequency of use. Thus, in day-to-day decision-making, the motorist considers the city streets free. More and more commuters use private automobiles rather than public-transit facilities. The resultant congestion leads to demands for heavy expenditures to improve the roads. This is a losing battle since the additional roads, again provided free to the motorist, further divert traffic from mass transit systems to private cars, further congestion, and further the need for more roads. Economists have long advocated that the commuter motorist pay the marginal cost he imposes on society, the cost of roads, plus his contribution to congestion. If he had to pay a substantial toll, the market test thus provided would indicate whether the pleasure of driving his own car into town was worth the social cost. Access roads might have toll stations, street permits could be issued, or parking could be made expensive.[7] But the practical men of the world have ruled out this solution, and so we can look forward to an endless cycle of congested highways, new construction at great cost, more motorists, more congestion.

IMPROVEMENTS IN THE DECISION-MAKING PROCESS

Economics can also be applied to design an institutional situation in which decision-makers are more likely to reach economically sound results. The revolution in the decision-making machinery of the Department of Defense shows several fundamental ways in which this can be done. The experience of the Defense Department should prove applicable to other fields, in both the public and the private sectors.

First, the organizational structure can be arranged in such a way that one decision unit is responsible for a given objective. In that way one authority is actually confronted with a choice among a full range of alternatives that can be used to achieve that objective and can rationally seek out the best one. For example, Polaris submarines and Minuteman missiles are alternative means for achieving strategic objectives. If key budget decisions are made within the Navy and within the Air Force, then Polaris competes with other ships and Minuteman missiles with airplanes, rather than having the two missile systems competing with each other. By concentrating this choice process in the hands of the Secretary of Defense, the possibility is created of systematically searching for the most effective, least-cost missile system, or for the best combination. In the absence of this kind of centralized choice, the outcome is likely to be determined by bureaucratic in-fighting and bargaining among agencies pushing their particular weapons systems.

In contrast, the development of the nation's water resources is in the hands of competing agencies in different departments, the Army Corps of Engineers in the Defense Department, the Bureau of Reclamation of the Department of the Interior, and other agencies. In the absence of one unified center of decision-making, there is no assurance that the best development is pursued on each river, as each agency promotes its particular purposes.

Second, the information must be organized so that the policy-makers face the most relevant choices. Until recently, for example, key decisions in the defense budget were primarily concerned with the division of the total

---

[7] Gasoline taxes do not provide a test because gasoline use does not correspond to the social costs of being on the highways during the peak periods.

budget among the Army, Navy, Air Force and Marines, not with accomplishing our several national defense objectives. The defense budget has now been converted to show how much is to be spent for each objective. The major weapons systems are grouped according to their military purposes. The Air Force Minuteman missiles are put together with the Navy's Polaris submarines and the other weapons designed for the strategic deterrent role. Table 5 gives the budget summary of this information. The division between the armed services does not appear. The table does not tell how much should be spent for each purpose, or indicate marginal benefits. But it does pose the problem in such a manner that the president knows how much is being spent for each purpose; he can then exercise his own judgment in deciding for what purposes additional outlays should be made. This budgeting approach also provides the general framework for seeking out the least-cost solutions within each purpose.

TABLE 5

Department of Defense Budget Program

Major Military Programs	1964 Estimate (in billions)
Strategic retaliatory forces	$ 7.3
Continental air and missile defense forces	2.0
General purpose forces	19.1
Sealift and airlift	1.4
Reserve forces	2.0
Research and development (not included elsewhere)	5.9
General support	14.6
Civil defense	0.3
Proposed legislation: military compensation increase	0.9
Total	53.6

Third, costs must be viewed over a number of years. For most programs the first-year cost is small, and all too frequently that is all that will be found in the budget. Costs of a program such as a new weapons system build up to a peak over several years, and if decision-making is to be rational, the total cost over the entire program life has to be considered, not just the initial year's expense. The Defense Department now operates on a 5-year budget, showing the time profile of the costs for each program; but these figures have not been made public. Outside of defense, comprehensive forward estimates are made by only a few small agencies, and this is one of the most serious shortcomings of the present budgetary process.

Fourth, decision-making is improved by creating an institutional setup under which the pressures on the decision-makers lead them in the direction of economic choices. In the private market economy self-interest and the discipline of the profit-and-loss statement serve to produce rational production decisions. In the public sector decision-makers do not maximize profits. Instead, they operate by the criteria which are imposed on them by the organization in which they operate. If the criteria are designed to promote the achievement of the public-policy objectives, a process not very different from the market mechanism will occur; if the criteria are badly designed, waste and failure will ensue. For example, military supply officers maintain inventories of clothing, ammunition, equipment, and the like. A "good" supply officer has the things his men need; a bad one is always running into shortages. Inevitably, supply officers become hoarders, eager to obtain as many supplies as they can to be ready for all contingencies. Under modern conditions, where weapons become obsolete rapidly, this hoarding produces waste. Inventories become too big, tie up capital, and many items become obsolete before they are used. A proper criterion for supply decisions takes account both of the losses suffered when an item is unavailable and the costs of stocking the items. In recent years the armed services have adopted such economic criteria, and supply officers are now judged not only by their skill in maintaining large inventories but also by their ability to keep the total costs down.

INCENTIVE CONTRACTS FOR GOVERNMENT PROCUREMENT

With the Defense Department spending close to $20 billion a year for the procurement of equipment, efficiency in procurement is particularly important. The government usually grants contracts to manufacturers to supply specific items. Where the item is standard and requires little technological novelty—such as uniforms, gasoline, tires, and food—contracts are let by competitive bidding after public notice. This assures a competitive result through the normal processes of the private economy. A large part of procurement, however, is for complicated equipment (missiles, and the like), frequently of a type that has never been manufactured before, and sometimes still requiring development. Here competitive bidding is impossible because the product cannot be precisely specified nor can there be assurance that the manufacturer will in fact succeed in producing it. In the past a "cost-plus" contract was used under which the manufacturers produced the item and the government agreed to pay whatever the cost turned out to be plus a fixed percentage for profits or a fixed fee. This system provides no incentive for the manufacturer to keep costs down; in fact, the higher the cost, the higher his profit. This is really backward economics! An alternative would be to offer the manufacturer a contract which specifies a fixed price, leaving any cost-saving wholly in the hands of the manufacturer as extra profit. This, after all, is the incentive which reduces costs in the private economy. But this approach is not feasible where the costs are as unknown as they are in advanced weaponry, for the government would have to offer private companies a very high price to make it worthwhile for them to run the large risks that the fixed-price contract would entail. It is not uncommon for weapons systems to cost more than twice as much as originally expected. Nor is there any assurance that technical specifications can be met at any price.

To steer a middle path between removing all incentives for cost-cutting and having to pay very high risk premiums, the government has experimented with incentive contracts, under which the manufacturer may keep a fraction of any cost-saving below the original estimate, and is penalized by a fraction of any excesses of costs above the estimates. Such contracts are no substitute for the normal workings of competition, but at least they introduce some incentives to keep costs down rather than to inflate them. On-time delivery and technical quality have also been promoted by incentive contracts.

Concluding Notes: the Political Reality

The study of the economics of public expenditures is still in its infancy, and it would be rash indeed to evaluate the present decision processes in terms of the ideals of economic theory. But here are a few observations on the actual process.

1. Present decisions rely heavily on the activities of pressure groups at several stages of the budget cycle both in the executive branch and the Congress. Lobbying is a highly organized activity in this country, and many public needs are brought to public attention by this process. But programs which would help the unorganized are likely to be stinted.

2. An old program is a good program. Once it has existed for a period, a program generates its own clientele, both inside and outside the government, which has a vested interest in its continuance. With total spending possibilities always outrunning likely revenues, new programs encounter difficult sledding.

3. Our political system gives more groups the power to exercise vetoes than to initiate new programs. For a program to get started, it must not only have the positive backing of lots of people, but it must encounter relatively few vetoes. (This is illustrated by our failure to enact general aid to education after two decades of awareness of need. On the other hand, our highway programs have been greatly expanded because they have strong backing by some groups and little opposition.)

4. Bargaining is an important part of decision-making. There is bargaining between rival government agencies, between the Bureau of the Budget and the operating agencies, between the president and the congressional committees, and among representatives of different regions and other groups within the Congress. The viewpoints of interested parties are also expressed through congressional hearings and informal lobbying. This process of bargaining is untidy and follows no simple, logical principles. But it does usually guarantee that important issues are not overlooked. It cuts down the kind of gross mistakes which the more efficient decision processes of totalitarian governments occasionally produce.

Summary

Expenditure decisions in the public sector are reached through the budgeting process. A budget contains the planned expenditures and revenues for a fiscal year. The federal government has a highly sophisticated budgeting process, in which the detailed requests of spending agencies are weighed against the needs of over-all fiscal policy.

Three sets of budget figures are currently in use in the U.S. The Administrative Budget is the traditional budget and has a legal basis. However, it leaves out trust fund transactions. The Consolidated Cash Budget is comprehensive, including all transactions. The National Income and Product Account Budget allocates receipts to the period when their economic impact is felt, and leaves out expenditures which do not use up resources or add to private incomes.

Economic principles can be applied to budgeting to improve the efficiency of resource allocation in the public sector. The principle that marginal benefit must exceed marginal cost can be applied in some limited fields. But for a large part of government expenditures, no objective measure of benefit can be defined. The principle that objectives be met with the least-cost method can be applied more widely, particularly in the defense field. Economic pricing of marketable public services also can help to assure an efficient use of resources.

To achieve rational choices, the decision-making process must be properly designed. Relevant alternatives for accomplishing each objective must be weighed against one another. Expenditures must be clearly identified with the objectives they are to accomplish. The pressures on decision-makers must be of the sort that will lead to the application of proper criteria. And costs over the entire period of a program, not just for 1 year, have to be taken into account.

3

THE PUBLIC FINANCES
OF STATE AND LOCAL GOVERNMENTS

Chapter 1 wrestled with the question: What activities should be carried out publicly rather than privately? Once the scope of public activity is defined, it remains to decide on the proper division of activity among the several levels of government in our federal system—what should be done by the federal government, what by state and local governments.

In some New England towns, the open town meeting, with every citizen eligible to vote, is still the prevailing legislature. Here is pure democracy. When it comes to public finance, the residents of the town register their own judgments about the benefits and cost of expenditures. The town administrators may submit their budgets, but the town meeting usually has ideas of its own which keep the government efficient and the cost low.

When you contrast this decision-making process with Washington or the state capitals—with legislators dealing with a wide range of issues, many of them remote from their own experience, pressured by lobbyists seeking benefits without costs for their group, imposing common policies on a wide range of communities of different circumstances and desires—you see the advantage of having a federal system, with vigorous local governments to handle what problems they can.

The federal government has become bigger and more powerful as compared to governments at state and local levels in this century. But in public spending, state and local governments have remained important, and in fact, are experiencing a great resurgence. Since the end of the Korean War, increases in state and local expenditures have been much greater than federal expenditures. The task of providing education for a rapidly rising school-age population has been left almost wholly at the state and local level. Other costs have risen as well—for roads, sewers, hospitals, water supply, public assistance, and police and fire protection. In a few cases, the federal government has made grants-in-aid to help meet the cost, leaving administration to the states and localities. In fact, of all the public services other than those connected with foreign policy (defense, foreign aid, space, etc.) the state and local governments today provide much the larger part.

One of the most intriguing problems of the economics of public finance is to determine the level of government most appropriate for handling each of the public services. This chapter deals with that question, and then takes up the general finance problems confronting state and local governments.

The Advantages of Local Government

Many people feel that whatever can be done privately, should be, and if it must be done by government, that it be at the local level, or as a second choice, by the states. This view is based on the belief that the total power of government should be kept as small as possible to protect the individual and private institutions, and that power in our society remain diffused rather than centralized. Furthermore, only the exercise of governmental functions keeps local governments healthy, and it is they which provide the main opportunity for individual participation in government. Washington is far removed from the daily lives of most of us. We vote for presidents and congressmen, but that is very different from voting in a New England town meeting, or serving on a school board, or running for local alderman. These are political reasons but they have their economic counterparts.

1. Expenditure decisions may be made more rationally in a small government than in a big one, because of the greater coincidence between the distribution of the benefits and costs. In the case of a proposed new federal program, individuals—and their congressmen—take less cognizance of the resultant increase in taxes because the share which they or their district will have to pay will be small. In local government the resultant tax cost usually can be seen more immediately by the taxpayers. Even in local government, collective choices made through the political process are not subject to the

market test. But when decisions are made for a small community, other things being equal, the rational market result is more likely to be approximated because judgment is apt to be better informed and the possibilities of non-beneficiaries paying are smaller.   1309928

2. A multiplicity of separate communities creates the possibility of some individual choice even about collective goods. You recall from Chapter 1 that one of the characteristics of a collective good was that all the members of the community had to enjoy the same level of the good regardless of their individual desires, simply because it was supplied jointly to all of them. Where there are many communities involved, a new kind of choice is introduced. Each individual can elect to become a member of that community which offers him the combination of collective goods which he prefers. For example, in the typical metropolitan area with its core city and its numerous suburbs, one man may prefer to have his family live in a community which has excellent schools but high taxes; another, perhaps the head of a childless family or with children beyond school age, may prefer a poor school system and low taxes. Now, since a person can only live in one place, he cannot pick the precise combination of public services he prefers, but at least he has some choice about their general pattern. This process of community selection produces an even greater coincidence of benefits and costs in public services. Typically, families who have a stake in education flock together in the suburbs, as do older couples or families who prefer not to send their children to public schools. Each receives the school system that he wants and is willing to pay for.

3. Even more important, decentralizing public functions at the state and local level permits each region to apply its own values to government programs. Unlike some of the smaller and more homogenous countries of Europe, the people in different parts of the United States have quite different ideas about the proper public responsibility in such fields as public assistance and unemployment benefits, about the nature of education, and even about the proper division between the private and the public sectors. Whatever government services are supplied at the state and local level can be provided in accordance with regional preferences; the national government must impose uniform standards if it is to undertake a program.

4. Decentralization also permits experimentation and pioneering by a few communities, which later on may set the standards for the rest of the country. Compare the American educational system with centralized systems in Western Europe and Japan. Here, the federal government has virtually no voice; state education departments are powerful in determining the curricula and setting standards in some parts of the country, while elsewhere the decision-making power is kept in the local school board. As a result, some schools are superlative, developing new teaching techniques, changing curricula with the needs of the times, and employing well-paid, highly qualified teachers. Other school systems vary from very good to downright poor, depending on the attitudes and the economic resources of the communities and states. In a country such as France, power is concentrated in the Ministry of Education, which determines curricula, picks textbooks, trains and hires teachers, even sets nationwide examinations for the students. The result is a greater uniformity among school systems, with less innovation and few schools of true excellence, but with fairly good schools even if the community is poor and does not value education highly.

5. The political process by which spending decisions are reached in some cases imposes a spending pattern on programs which reflects the distribution of political power rather than any rational economic criteria. At the federal level there is an important regional element to the distribution of power, and hence of public money. Whatever the general objectives of a program may be, there will be strong pressures to allocate funds in a regional pattern which reflects political reality. Expenditures at the local level also go through some similar log-rolling, but the possibilities are more limited.

The Advantages of National Programs

The United States was originally established because of the need for a national government. Looked at from the limited perspective of economics, here are some of the factors requiring national action:

1. Certain public services are collective for the country as a whole, in the sense that they are provided jointly for all the individuals of the nation. Defense and other programs in support of our foreign policy are clearly of this character. Other public services are collective to a smaller community and thus can be provided through a government including the smaller group. Police and fire protection are examples.

2. Some public services involve the national interest to some degree, but not exclusively so, and reasonable men can differ whether the national interest is sufficient to justify national programs. For example, the entire society has a stake in the education of its citizens. We all share the same political process, the quality of which depends on an educated citizenry. The cultural richness of our society as well as our effectiveness in accomplishing such tasks as the space effort and defense, depend on the quality of our education. And we all enjoy higher incomes because our labor force has a high average degree of education. Are these factors sufficient to make education a national concern? So far the country has decided on a qualified "No," with national programs confined to limited financial support of science in the schools and of higher education.

3. The superiority of the financial resources of the federal government tends to cause programs to gravitate to the national level. The federal government has appropriated some of the best revenue sources, particularly income taxation, and this has made it difficult for the state and local governments to find adequate funds. Competition among states for new industry has also limited the use of some taxes, especially taxes on business. Furthermore, average incomes are much higher in some states than in others. If a minimum level of a public service is to be assured everywhere, the wealthier states must help out the poorer states, as they do when the federal tax is used for financing.

4. The willingness to undertake public services is sometimes greater at the national than at the state and local level. (Not everybody would consider this a virtue.) Although the same individuals elect officials at the several levels of government, the political choices that are made on spending matters will not necessarily be the same. Locally, heavily taxed property owners, who are not likely to be sympathetic to spending, may be particularly influential. Also, our most important media of mass communication are national, and hence it is easier to arouse popular interest in a problem or a need on a nationwide rather than a local basis. Our attention is focused on Washington, not on our state capitals or on our cities and towns.

5. Finally, many state and local governments are just plain inefficient and lack initiative. They find it difficult to attract top quality personnel with the salaries they offer. In some areas corruption is a serious problem. Even though many of the economic challenges to government in the present decade are at the state and local level—in such fields as education, urban renewal, and resource development—the leadership necessary to formulate effective programs is all too often lacking locally.

Post-War Financing of State and Local Governments

We have already seen in Chapter 1 that the total expenditures of state and local governments have increased enormously in the post-war period, more than in any other sector of the economy. Total outlays were $27.9 billion in 1950, but by 1961 they had reached $55.8 billion. No one would have predicted that state and local governments would prove capable of financing such enormous outlays, given the relatively low response of their taxes to income growth. Such increases would have struck most experts as impossible; and in fact, a general financial crisis for state and local governments has been predicted repeatedly. Yet, in most areas, the revenue requirements have been met; Table 6 summarizes how it was accomplished.

The property tax, which had long been assumed not to respond to economic growth, yielded more than twice as much as it had 11 years earlier,

TABLE 6

Total Revenues and Expenditures
of State and Local Governments 1950-1961 (Billions of dollars)

	1950	State and Local 1961	Percentage Increase
Revenues			
Total	20.9	54.0	158
Property taxes	7.3	18.0	147
Sales and excise taxes	5.2	12.4	138
Individual income taxes	.8	2.6	225
Corporation income taxes	.6	1.3	117
Other taxes	2.0	4.5	125
Charges and miscellaneous revenues	2.5	8.0	220
Revenues from Federal Government	2.5	7.1	184
Expenditures			
Total	22.8	56.3	146
Education	7.2	20.6	186
Highways	3.8	9.8	158
Public welfare	2.9	4.7	62
Hospitals and health	1.7	4.1	141
Police and fire	1.3	3.1	138
Sewerage and sanitation	.8	1.8	125
Parks and resources	1.0	2.2	120
Interest	.5	1.8	260
All others (housing, prisons, airports, libraries, administration, etc.)	3.6	8.1	125

Source: Bureau of the Census, U.S. Department of Commerce.

because of the growth of the tax base associated with the post-war building boom and substantially raised rates and improved administration. It had always been difficult to administer the tax, particularly in periods of inflation, when frequent, thoroughly unpopular, reassessment of property values is necessary in order for the tax to keep pace with the price level. Nevertheless, in the face of the acute financial need, many communities did reassess to increase the size of the base, and also increased the rates steadily.

Revenues from sales taxes also increased very sharply, partly in response to economic growth, partly due to the adoption of general sales taxes in additional states, as well as increases in rates. Similarly, state income taxes, both individual and corporate, experienced large increases. Other taxes, such as the excises on alcohol, tobacco, and gasoline, were also raised in most places.

Grant-in-aid programs from the federal government also helped significantly, rising from $2.5 to $7.1 billion. The federal government took over the financing of much of the highway program and also increased its contribution to state and local public-welfare programs, in both cases leaving administration at the state and local level.

State Tax Systems

Not all states have met their financial problems in the same way. Table 7 is a summary of the 50 state tax systems, indicating what taxes are imposed and their basic rates. You can see that there are substantial differences in state tax patterns, both in the kinds of taxes levied and in the rates. These differences reflect to some extent the characteristics of the states' economies, differences in history and tradition, and differences in local preferences.

What about the future? By 1970 state and local expenditures may well exceed $100 billion a year. Their tax systems are likely to cover most of this increase. But it will mean repeated increases in tax rates, perhaps the introduction of income and sales taxes in additional states, as their financial position remains under steady pressure. Federal grants will also rise to some extent.

The financial problem will also differ among the states. Economic resources are not distributed uniformly. Per-capita personal income in 1962 was below $1,715 in the poorest 8 states, above $2,775 in the richest 8.

A semi-official recent study [1] gives estimates of the revenues that a representative tax system, uniformly applied in all states, would yield. This system, an average of U.S. state tax systems, would yield from $231 to $325 per capita in the top 8 states, from $115 to $144 in the bottom 8 states. At the same time, some of the poorest states have particularly large proportions of school children and of destitute families.

Solutions to the Problems of State and Local Finance

Since we prefer activities to be carried on locally, several proposals have been made to help the financial situation of the state and local governments.

[1] Advisory Commission on Intergovernmental Relations, *Measures of State and Local Fiscal Capacity and Tax Effort* (October, 1962), p. 54.

RETURNING FUNCTIONS AND TAXES TO THE STATES

President Eisenhower was particularly sympathetic to this problem. He appointed the Kestnbaum Commission [2] which thoroughly studied the whole range of issues involving federal-state-local fiscal relationships. This commission urged greater federal-state cooperation but did not propose any drastic changes in present arrangements. Subsequent to their report, Eisenhower set up a Joint Federal-State Action Committee of governors and federal officials to determine a new distribution of functional responsibilities and the corresponding adjustment of revenues. This group finally recommended, after studying many programs, that responsibility for vocational education and for waste-treatment facilities be returned to the states and that a part of the federal telephone tax be repealed in order to be reimposed by the states. It was interesting that this group was not able to come up with other proposals. It turned out that the distribution of the benefits of returning a tax to the states was always different from the distribution of the costs, and therefore some states would be opposed. Furthermore, the officials managing the programs financed by grants-in-aid were fearful that the states would not maintain their support. The modest proposal which was recommended and which surrendered more of the federal tax base than the costs of the returned programs, was sent by the president to Congress, but was not enacted into law. Thus, when the issue of turning functions back to the states was put to the test of the political process both at the state and federal level, it turned out that people were quite content to have Washington do it.

BLOCK GRANTS

Block grants are another proposal designed to strengthen state finances while leaving control decentralized. The federal government would simply turn over a fixed annual grant to the states, helping their financial situation without influencing decisions. Any additional expenditures which state legislatures might vote would have to be completely financed out of their own tax sources. Such grants could be of several forms. They could take the form of *tax-sharing*—that is, each state would receive a grant equal to some fraction of the revenues which the federal government collects in the state, say under the income tax. This method would be free of the taint of subsidy, since in some sense, the state would only receive back what was collected from it in the first place. But tax-sharing does not equalize fiscal capabilities, since the poor states would receive the smallest grants. Alternatively, one could enact *equalizing grants*, based on a formula such as per-capita income or fiscal capacity. *Consolidated grants* have also been proposed, under which the federal government totals up the sums of money it now grants to each state under the more than 100 specific grant-in-aid programs in force. By converting these specific grants into one irrevocable consolidated amount, federal control would be removed.[3]

---

[2] The Commission on Intergovernmental Relations, *A Report to the President for Transmittal to the Congress*, June, 1955.

[3] See George C. S. Benson and Harold F. McClelland, *Consolidated Grants: A Means of Maintaining Fiscal Responsibility* (Washington, D.C.: American Enterprise Association, December, 1961). The first Hoover Commission (1949) On Organization of the Executive Branch of the Government favored consolidating grants into a few "broad categories, such as highways, education, public assistance, and public health—as contrasted with the present system of extensive fragmentation." *Report on Federal-State Relations*, p. 36.

TABLE 7

State Tax System 1963

	General Sales and Gross Receipts (rate) (1)	Individual Income Taxes (max. rates) (2)	Corporation Income Taxes (max. rates) (3)	Selective Excise Taxes			Other Major Taxes (7)
				Motor Fuel (¢ per gal.) (4)	Tobacco (¢ per 20 cigs.) (5)	Alcoholic Beverages (per gal. unless stated otherwise) (6)	
Alabama	4	5	3	7	6	30% of retail	
Alaska	.5	16% of fed. tax	18% of fed. tax	8	8	$4	Raw fish tax (tax on fishing gear and value of fish)
Arizona	3	4.5	5	6	2	$1.44	
Arkansas	3	5	5	6.5	6	$2.50	
California	3	7	5.5	6	3	$1.50	
Colorado	2	8	5	6	—	$1.80	
Connecticut	3.5	—	5	6	5	$2.00	
Delaware	.14	11	5	6	5	$1.15	
District of Columbia	3	5	5	6	2	$1.50	
Florida	3	—	—	7	5	$2.40	
Georgia	3	6	4	6.5	5	$1.00	
Hawaii	3.5	9	5.5	11	20% of wholesale price	16% of wholesale price	
Idaho	—	10.5	10.5	6	7	S.L.C. + 10%	
Illinois	3.5	—	—	5	4	$1.52	
Indiana	2	—	—	6	4	$2.00	
Iowa	2	3.75	3	6	4	10%	
Kansas	2.5	5.5	3.5	5	4	$2.40	
Kentucky	3	6	7	7	2.5	$1.28	
Louisiana	2	6	4	7	—	$1.58	Severance tax (tax on production of coal, oil, gas, etc.)
Maine	4	—	—	7	6	S.L.C. + $1	
Maryland	3	5	5	6	6	$1.50	
Massachusetts	—	7.4	6.8	5.5	6	$2.25	
Michigan	4	—	—	6	7	8%	
Minnesota	—	10.5	9.3	5	7	$2.50	

State						Amount	Notes
Mississippi	3	6	6	7	8	"dry" state	
Missouri	3	4	2	5	4	$1.20	
Montana	–	7	4.5	6	8	20%	
Nebraska	–	–	–	7	4	$1.20	
Nevada	2	–	–	6	4	$1.40	
New Hampshire	–	4.25	–	7	15% retail	S.L.C.	Parimutuel taxes (7% of total contribution to pools)
New Jersey	–	10	1.75	6	7	$1.80	
New Mexico	3	6	3	6	8	$1.50	Severance tax (minerals, oil and gas)
New York	–	10	5.5	6	5	$1.50	
North Carolina	3	7	6	7	–	12%	
North Dakota	2.25	11	6	6	3	$2.65	
Ohio	3	3	–	7	5	$1.00	
Oklahoma	2	6	4	6.58	7	$2.40	Gross production tax (on minerals, oil and gas)
Oregon	–	9.5	6	6	–	S.L.C.	
Pennsylvania	5	–	6	7	6	10%	
Rhode Island	3	–	6	7	6	$2.00	
South Carolina	3	7	5	7	5	$4.00	
South Dakota	2	–	–	6	6	$2.50	
Tennessee	3	6	4	7	7	$2.50	
Texas	2	–	–	5	4	$1.68	Severance tax (oil, gas sulphur, cement)
Utah	3	5	4	6	8	S.L.C. + 4%	
Vermont	–	7.5	5	6.5	7	$5.10	
Virginia	–	5	5	7	3	10%	
Washington	4	–	–	7.5	4	S.L.C. + 10%	
West Virginia	2	5.5	–	7	6	S.L.C.	
Wisconsin	3	8.5	7	6	6	$2.00	
Wyoming	2	–	–	5	4	$ .80	
No. Using Tax	40	36	37	51	47	50	

Source: State and Local Taxes, Prentice-Hall, Englewood Cliffs, N. J.
(S.L.C. = State Liquor Commission.)

Canada has an extensive system of block grants to the provinces, which admittedly has led to considerable political bickering about the amounts, but which has worked fairly well. Great Britain has used them in limited amounts to help local governments. In the United States the Congress has not been sympathetic to the approach, nor did the Kestnbaum Commission favor it. Congress prefers to give grants to accomplish specific national purposes, to get the state and local governments to initiate or extend activities which they would not otherwise undertake. Presumably the political body which imposes the taxes must also have some responsibility for the manner in which they are spent.

As a result, we have an elaborate system of *conditional grants-in-aid*. Some are *matching grants*, in which the federal government puts up, say, 50 per cent of the funds for a program if the state government raises the other 50 per cent; this leaves some of the cost for every program with the state, and makes state governments consider at least part of the tax cost in their spending decisions. In other cases, grants may allocate fixed amounts without matching funds, to assure minimum standards. For example, federal grants for some type of public assistance may provide all of the first $14 per week per recipient, with any benefits that the state decides to pay beyond that level having to be financed by the state itself.

Summary

A federal, or multi-level, system of government has important advantages over a centralized system. It permits a greater diffusion of power, more sensitive choices about collective goods, the application of different values in programs in different regions and localities, and great opportunity for experimentation.

On the other hand, some of the most important public services deal with collective goods for the country as a whole, involving the national interest, and ought to be undertaken nationally. The federal government also has superior financial resources. Lack of local initiative makes us undertake some programs at the national level, even though they really deal with local problems. Years of inquiries by presidential commissions and other groups have produced no results in returning expenditure functions to the states.

State and local expenditures have increased enormously in the post-war period. These expenditures have largely been financed out of state and local resources. Tax rates have been increased and new taxes adopted. Grant-in-aid programs from the federal government have also helped, but in a minor way.

The fiscal capacity of the 50 states varies widely, and this fact, together with the expectation of another doubling of local expenditures in the next 10 years, has led to various proposals to provide additional financial aid from the federal to state and local governments. Most of these proposals seek to provide financial assistance while preserving local control. So far, however, the Congress has preferred to help states and localities through conditional grants for specific programs, designed to foster certain lines of expenditure.

4

ECONOMICS OF METROPOLITAN AREAS

Sixty-three per cent of the American people now live in metropolitan areas. As defined by the Census Bureau, the country has 212 standard metropolitan areas (SMA's) which range from the largest, the New York area with 15 million people, to San Angelo, Texas, with 65 thousand. Over 60 million live in areas of a size greater than 1 million; almost 100 million in SMA's greater than 500,000. Each area is a cluster of communities, usually consisting of a central core city plus surrounding suburbs. The growth of these areas and the

43

large percentage of our population which now lives in them is a measure of the extent to which America has become urbanized (see Table 8).

Metropolitan areas have been defined not on the basis of legal boundaries of units of government, but according to economic integration. People live and work within each area, often not in the same town. Thus, there is an immense amount of movement among the towns within the area. People do their shopping, seek much of their recreation, and have their friends all within the area. Clearly, each area needs an efficient transportation system for the movement of people and goods at high speed and low cost. Most metropolitan areas are encountering serious difficulties in this task.

The communities in a metropolitan area have other common economic problems. A sensible division of the land among residential, commercial,

TABLE 8

Population Growth of 22 Standard Metropolitan Areas
(With population over 1 million in 1960)

	Population of Area (in thousands)	
	1900	1960
Atlanta	141	1,017
Baltimore	578	1,727
Boston	1,250	2,589
Buffalo	394	1,310
Chicago-N.W. Indiana	1,851	6,794
Cincinnati	496	1,072
Cleveland	420	1,797
Dallas	43	1,084
Detroit	317	3,762
Houston	45	1,243
Kansas City	285	1,039
Los Angeles-Long Beach	123	6,743
Milwaukee	325	1,194
Minneapolis-St. Paul	372	1,482
New York-N.E. New Jersey	4,718	14,759
Philadelphia	1,623	4,343
Pittsburgh	793	2,405
St. Louis	650	2,060
San Diego	40	1,033
San Francisco	473	2,783
Seattle	81	1,107
Washington	305	2,001
Total	15,324	63,344

Population of 22 Areas as a Percentage of U.S. Population

1900	1910	1920	1930	1940	1950	1960
20.2	22.8	25.2	30.6	32.2	33.9	35.5

Source: Bureau of the Census.

industrial, and recreational uses requires an area-wide point of view. The general prosperity of the population depends not on the town alone but on the prosperity of the area as a whole. Often, public services such as sewers, hospitals, police and fire protection, and even libraries and schools can be provided more efficiently on an area-wide basis. In the economist's jargon, the typical area is a nest of spill-overs, of physical interdependence, and of economies and diseconomies external to individual communities. The boundaries of the local governments within the metropolitan area fail to correspond to the proper boundaries for rational planning and decision-making and the efficient supply of many government services.

Metropolitan areas today pose some of the most interesting, not to say perplexing, problems in public finance. The important issues of local expenditures and taxation cannot meaningfully be considered without some analysis of the economics of metropolitan areas. This chapter will chiefly be concerned with one question: How can public services be organized most effectively in the modern metropolitan area?

Trouble in the Core City

Our large cities, which are the heart of the metropolitan areas, have all experienced a gradual process of physical and economic deterioration. Manufacturing industry has been moving out. It had first been attracted to the city by the proximity of the railroads and a steady labor supply; but the rise of trucking, and now of airfreight, has made locations along major highways (and airports) outside the core city more attractive. This trend was accelerated by technical changes in factory buildings. Business found that modern one-story plants could operate at lower costs than the older multistory plants, but land values are too high in the city to make large one-story plants practical.

The cities have also been losing middle- and upper-income families to the suburbs. Partly a result of people's desire for more space and home-ownership, this movement accelerated when the cities became caught in a vicious spiral of spreading slums, rising crime, and worsening congestion. Once a neighborhood began to deteriorate, it did not pay any one landlord to maintain his own building, all of which led to a cumulative worsening of conditions. If all landlords invested in the upkeep of their property, neighborhoods might be preserved. But once decline sets in, the private return on investment becomes small, since little extra rent can be charged for the better kept-up buildings. This perhaps is the worst of the external diseconomies working against the preservation of our cities. The process was accentuated by the housing shortages after World War II, which made it easy to rent rundown apartments, and by the artificial shortages created by racial discrimination in housing, which preserves a captive market for dilapidated slum buildings in the large cities all over the United States. As a result, the tendency has been for only two groups of people to remain in the cities—the very rich who can afford to live in luxury apartments, especially if they are childless, and the poor, especially minorities, who have no choice but to live in the limited housing available to them and in close proximity to their unskilled jobs.

This process has created a difficult financial situation for the cities. On the one hand, they have to bear public assistance payments and other welfare costs for the low-income groups in the slums, as well as to continue to provide mass transportation, fire and police protection, and education. On the other hand, their tax base has failed to expand correspondingly as the high and middle income groups and industry fled the city.

Problems in the Suburbs

Meantime, the burgeoning suburbs have developed some problems of their own. In some of them population doubled and redoubled in a few years as developers put up moderate-scaled houses by the thousands. These communities had no financial resources of their own other than revenues from property taxes, and these were not equal to the enormous costs of providing schools and teachers for the numerous children of young families, as well as heavy initial investments for water supply, roads, and sewers. Some towns have sought to broaden their tax base by attracting industry. But as towns have competed for the new industries, they have made tax concessions which grant new industry partial exemption from the property taxes, thus reducing the total tax base of the area.

Taxes were high for other reasons as well: (1) There are some costs involved in being a separate unit of government—the town hall, a salaried mayor or city manager, perhaps a local court. (2) Some public services are carried on more efficiently on a larger scale. (3) Unless there is active grass-roots democracy with heavy citizen participation and responsibility, local government may be inefficient because of the difficulty of attracting top-flight administrative talent.

While some suburbs suffered from mediocre schools and from high tax rates, others became "tax havens." They required house lots to be so large and made building codes so complicated that it became very difficult to build new houses and hence to add to the school population. By these and other devices, they kept themselves islands of low tax rates.

Problems of Coordination and Planning:
Physical Interdependence Ignored

The division of the metropolitan area into many legal communities makes it particularly difficult to provide those public services for which the metropolitan area has to be considered a unit for physical reasons. It makes no sense to plan transportation on other than an area-wide basis because of the typically long distances separating people's homes from their places of work. A rational road network must be able to move cars freely within the area. Mass-transit systems, subways or buses, also should be laid out on an area-wide basis. Yet, it is usually only the core city which feels it has sufficient stake in such a system to give it active support; the commuter suburbs are happy to have residents drive into the city and then to let the city worry about the congestion of streets and downtown parking.

Water supply is a similar problem. To obtain a supply of high quality water at low cost frequently requires the construction of a large reservoir at some distance up in the mountains. In the absence of unified area planning, localities improvise their own supplies, out of wells or other sources. The ground water level may gradually fall as supplies are depleted. The pumping process slowly raises pumping costs to the town and neighboring communities. Having made the investment in the pumping facilities, they are slow to abandon them, and are reluctant to participate in building a cheaper, better common system.

The disposal of sewage is an even worse case. Some suburbs, particularly if they have been growing rapidly and are straining their resources to finance schools, provide no sewers. Their home-owners use septic tanks which discharge waste material into the ground. Even if they have sewers, the contents may be discharged into neighboring streams rather than treatment plants. This process has gone so far in some parts of the country that swimming at local beaches or streams has become impossible because of pollution. Even water supplies have been polluted by sewage seeping into the ground water.

These cases illustrate the point that the scope of particular governments must match the physical contours of the problems. Decentralization and local control are all very well, but not for the planning of water supplies and sewage disposal within a metropolitan area. When physical interdependence is ignored, decentralized decision-making does not lead to efficient results. The costs which localities consider in their choices are not the full social costs to the area.

Metropolitan Consolidation?

Observers who have watched some of these difficulties, particularly officials struggling vainly to gain adherence to area-wide plans for common facilities, have frequently proposed that a new level of government be set up which would embrace the entire metropolitan area. Such a government could rationally plan highways and mass-transit facilities, water supplies and sewage disposal, parks and beaches, the location of schools, even civil defense. It could also impose a common level of taxation, and would end the possibility of upper-income people and industry fleeing into "tax havens." Equipped with an adequate tax base and a proper span of control, such a government could, at least in principle, deal properly with the many problems of coordinated physical planning, and would have a better base for financing education and welfare programs. It could also supply some public services more efficiently.

Many of the issues involved in metropolitan consolidation are philosophical. Each person has to reach his own conclusion whether the improved planning and cost-savings are worth the increased centralization. But two issues can be analyzed more concretely. First, how large are the economies of scale for the various public services; second, what alternative solutions are there which would permit some of the advantages to accrue without the disadvantages?

Several statistical studies have been made of the costs of public services in communities of different sizes. In a study of the communities in the area of St. Louis, Missouri,[1] it was found that there were no measurable economies of scale in police protection, fire protection, education, and refuse collection. Administrative services enjoyed economies of scale at least up to medium-sized communities of 50,000-100,000 persons. Water and sewage services exhibited important economies of scale, with no evidence of diseconomies even for the largest systems. Studies of this type cannot be wholly conclusive, because one can argue that the higher (or at least no lower) costs of education

[1] Werner Z. Hirsch, "Expenditure Implications of Metropolitan Growth and Consolidation," *Review of Economics and Statistics*, Vol. XLI (August, 1959), pp. 232-241.

and other services of the large units are due to higher quality (which we cannot measure precisely), so that the taxpayer still receives more per dollar. But these studies do raise very serious doubts about across-the-board metropolitan consolidation justified primarily by economies of scale.

Apart from the statistical evidence, the efficiency argument for consolidation stumbles, at least in some places, on a more obvious obstacle. Many core-city governments, which could be expected to dominate the consolidated metropolitan area, are corrupt. To consolidate would mean to turn over well-run communities to the control of city machines. One can understand why suburbanites prefer some inefficiency and the costs of imperfect coordination to the prospect of falling under the sway of big-city politicians.

Alternatives to Metropolitan Consolidation

In fact, metropolitan consolidation has been carried out only to a very limited extent. Toronto, Canada, consolidated in 1952 and had a successful subsequent experience of improved services, better coordination, and cost-savings. This example raised interest in the plan in other cities. Dade County, Florida, which has Miami as its core, was organized as a metropolitan government in 1957, and was given the tasks of supplying such public services as water, sewage, hospitals, welfare, parks, mass transit, urban renewal, and arterial roads. Nashville undertook a major consolidation in 1962. Elsewhere, as in Cleveland, St. Louis, Memphis, Albuquerque, and Louisville, voters defeated plans for consolidation even though these plans gave the proposed governments only limited functions. Typically, it was the resistance of the suburbs which defeated the proposals.[2]

In the absence of consolidation, some other solutions have been found, which at least eliminate some of the worst anomalies of the lack of unified political responsibility for common problems. First, some economies of scale have been realized through voluntary cooperation of communities. Regional high schools, shared incinerators, and mutual assistance agreements among fire departments are quite common. Some towns buy services from other communities. This technique has been most developed in the Los Angeles area, where Los Angeles County is almost a department store of public services; each town can contract to purchase virtually any service it wishes. When the city of Lakewood was formed in 1954, it decided to contract for all its public services except education, and this scheme is now known as the "Lakewood Plan."

Second, new governments, sometimes called Metropolitan Special Districts, or Authorities, have been created to supply specific government services. For example, the Los Angeles Metropolitan Water District provides much of the water supply to Southern California. The New York Port Authority, in addition to managing the port and bus terminals, builds and operates tunnels, bridges, and airports. It has an annual investment budget of over $100 million, which it finances partly out of its very lucrative tunnel and bridge tolls and partly out of bonds issued on its own credit. The Seattle Metropolitan Municipal Corporation takes care of sewage and pollution

___

[2] Up to 1920, the cities were able to keep the metropolitan population inside their boundaries by legally annexing the surrounding countryside. Local opposition brought this process to a halt.

control for its area. The Massachusetts Metropolitan District Commission supplies water, sewers, as well as some of the highways and parks of the Greater Boston area. There are also many smaller special districts, supplying smaller regions with water, sewerage, or some other service.

These governments have often proved highly efficient, though they are subject neither to the check of competition nor of the ballot box. They succeed in raising huge amounts of capital and seem to provide public services to the satisfaction of their consumers. They pose more difficult issues as political organisms. Although they are governments, possessing the power of eminent domain and sometimes even of taxation, they are certainly not democracies. Their chiefs are not elected by the residents of the area and are frequently appointed for such long terms that no elective official has any real check over them. In fact, in some areas, the technocrats who run these agencies are the most powerful politicians. Some of the facilities which they control, particularly tunnels, bridges, and toll roads, produce far more revenue than is required to repay the bonds on the specific facilities; the surplus becomes a pool of investible funds with which they search for new fields to conquer. With the regular governments perennially hard-pressed for tax money, more and more activities are turned over to them. America has not thought through the implications of this trend.

Third, some of the problems of metropolitan areas have been turned over to the federal government. The large cities particularly have found it impossible to cope with the problem of urban blight, as their tax resources have declined in relation to their mounting expenses. The federal urban renewal program is essentially a response to the failure of local jurisdictions to take effective action. Similarly, the federal highway program is providing an important share of the funds for building some of the main access arteries in metropolitan areas. The greatly expanded federal program of public assistance grants is providing important financial help for the welfare problems of the large cities. And limited grants for the improvement of mass-transit systems are now available for experimental purposes.

Until a few years ago, we did not view these urban problems in the perspective of total metropolitan areas. The radical solution of establishing a new level of government through metropolitan consolidation has not been, and is not likely to be, adopted widely. In some areas, we find *ad hoc* solutions, voluntary cooperation, new agencies, and a wholesale transfer of problems to the federal government. But these solutions are all piecemeal. They do not produce a rational, integrated transportation system for the metropolitan area as a whole, nor an equitable local tax system, nor a rational pattern of land use. We have a lot to learn in this area.[3]

Summary

Some of the most difficult problems of public finance today can be found in metropolitan areas. Because legal jurisdictions of governments do not coincide with economic boundaries, the proper provision of government

[3] This chapter draws on *Factors Affecting Voter Reactions to Governmental Reorganization in Metropolitan Areas*. Advisory Commission on Intergovernmental Relations, Washington, D.C., May, 1962; and *Alternative Approaches to Governmental Reorganization in Metropolitan Areas*, Advisory Commission on Intergovernmental Relations, Washington, D.C., June, 1962.

services requires some cooperation, coordination, and some centralized planning.

Almost 100 million people live in metropolitan areas with a population in excess of 500,000 people. The typical area contains a cluster of communities surrounding the central core city.

The core cities have been running into economic difficulties because of physical and economic deterioration. Industry and middle- and upper-income families have been leaving, eroding the tax base. Slums have sprung up as the private benefit of proper maintenance of apartment dwellings has fallen short of social benefit. It does not pay any one landlord to keep up his building as long as the rest of the neighborhood runs downhill.

Suburbs with rapidly rising populations have run into severe financial problems. Their tax resources are small in relation to their needs for new schools, water, roads, and sewers. In some instances individual suburbs are too small to be able to supply government services efficiently.

Decentralized planning cannot work properly if communities are physically interdependent. Transportation, water supply, and sewage disposal are three public services in which physical interdependence is particularly important, and in which an area-wide point of view is essential.

Consolidating communities in a metropolitan area under one government has been widely advanced to eliminate these problems. But so far, voters have rejected metropolitan consolidation in most popular referenda. Statistical studies suggest that economies of scale prevail for some services, particularly water and sewerage. But for many others, including education, there are little or no economies of scale, and hence metropolitan consolidation would not lead to substantial cost-savings.

To realize some of the advantages of consolidation without taking this major political step, a number of alternative arrangements have been introduced. These include voluntary cooperation among communities to provide common facilities, the "Lakewood Plan" under which communities can contract to purchase those government services which they feel they cannot produce efficiently themselves, and Metropolitan Special Districts, which are area-wide governments limited to providing certain specific government services.

The federal government has also been taking increasing responsibility for problems of urban areas, particularly through its urban renewal and highway programs.

5

TAXATION: PRINCIPLES
AND ISSUES OF FAIRNESS

Perhaps the most astonishing fact about the American tax system is the fantastic revenue that it collects; total taxes are over $150 billion, about 28% of gross national product. They are collected without violence or bloodshed, with only some mild griping.

This is a small miracle. It is possible because in our advanced society businesses and individuals keep accounting records from which they can compute their tax bill. More important, it is possible because, on the whole, people are willing to pay their taxes. Ours is a system of voluntary compliance, not of assessment and enforcement by government. Less than 2 per cent of the federal government's revenues are the direct result of Internal Revenue Service findings of underpayments. People know that the common costs of national defense, of educating our children, and of other necessary public services have to be met. Generally, people respect the law and pay their taxes.

For a voluntary system to work successfully, the people must be confident that taxes are levied fairly and that everyone pays his share. If the feeling becomes widespread that the tax system is simply a collection of loopholes and evasions, if people see their equally prosperous neighbors paying substantially less or enjoying tax-free expense account living, taxpayer morale declines. The submission of an honest tax return then ceases to be a simple act of morality. In many countries of the world, both rich and poor, ethics concerning taxes are separate from ethics in other spheres. In Italy and France, countries of old culture, the most respectable members of the business and professional classes will report a taxable income which is no more than a fraction of their true income. Businesses routinely keep two sets of books, one for their own use, the other for the tax collectors. We have been spared this Latin tradition. Willingness to pay taxes is one of the sources of our national strength. The fairness of our taxes, which is essential to the maintenance of our voluntary compliance system, is the central theme of this chapter.

The magnitude of the revenues raised also means that the performance of the economy is affected. These enormous payments cannot possibly leave the efficiency, growth, and stability of the economy unchanged. The manner in which these payments affect the economy will be discussed in subsequent chapters.

This chapter deals mostly with the federal tax system; state and local taxes were taken up, at least briefly, in Chapter 3. Before analyzing the system, we need some basic definitions and concepts.

Some Basic Concepts

TAX BASES AND TAX RATES

Every tax is composed of a base and of a rate structure applied to that base. The base is the object which is taxed. It may be personal or business income, the sale of salt (an important base in the Middle Ages) or of other commodities, the total volume of sales of a business, the value of property, the estate left by an individual, the crossing of goods over a frontier (tariffs), and so on. This base may be taxed at a flat rate, such as a percentage of value or a fixed amount per physical unit, or with a more elaborate rate structure, such as the progressive income tax rates.

SHIFTING AND INCIDENCE

Frequently, a tax is collected from one individual, while in fact it is someone else who pays. By adjusting his actions, the taxed individual may be able to escape part of the burden and shift it to someone else. For example, the federal tax on cigarettes is collected from the manufacturers, yet they do not really pay most of the tax. They raise the price of the cigarettes, so that they *shift* the tax *forward* to the consumer, who pays the tax through higher prices. The *incidence*—that is, the final resting place of the tax burden—in this case falls on the consumer. To some extent, the tax also may lower the demand for tobacco, resulting in a lower price paid to tobacco-growers. Thus, a little of the tax may be *shifted backward,* placing some of the incidence on the growers.[1]

Some Practical Criteria for Tax Systems

Both for the sake of fairness and for minimizing the damage done to the economy, a tax system should display sound administrative qualities. These include:

CERTAINTY

For a private economy to operate successfully, it needs a stable political environment, including a tax system under which payments are predictable. Investment is risky under the best of circumstances, and if business is uncertain about the amount of taxes that is to be paid, investment will be reduced. Similarly, individuals should be secure against unpredictable taxes levied on their wages or other incomes. The law should be clear and specific;

---

[1] The process of shifting can be illustrated through a simple diagram. Let S and D be the supply and demand curves of a commodity. p_1 is the initial equilibrium price, q_1 the equilibrium quantity. Now suppose an excise tax of a fixed amount per unit is imposed. Then the supply curve shifts upward by the amount of the tax, that is, to obtain any given amount of the good, buyers must offer a greater price, including tax, to draw forth the supply. But at higher prices they demand less, and so a new equilibrium is found at q_2, where consumers pay p_2, producers receive p_3, and the difference between p_2 and p_3 is the tax which goes to the government.

In example (a) the larger part of the tax was passed on in a higher price, the smaller part was absorbed by the producers. But suppose the demand were a lot more elastic, and the supply less elastic, as in (b). Then more of the incidence falls on the suppliers. In the limiting case where the supply is completely inelastic, i.e., fixed, the whole of the tax will fall on the suppliers, example (c). Conversely, if the demand is completely inelastic, the tax will be completely shifted forward.

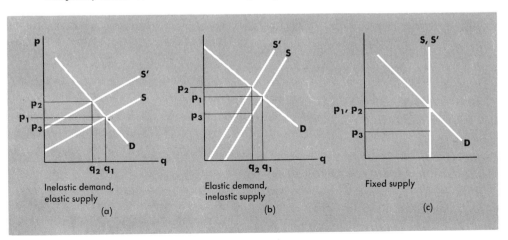

Inelastic demand, elastic supply

(a)

Elastic demand, inelastic supply

(b)

Fixed supply

(c)

tax collectors should have little discretion about how much to assess tax-payers, for this is a very great power and subject to abuse.

In our present tax system, the property tax based on arbitrary, local assessments of value is probably the most uncertain tax, and for this reason leads to a great deal of friction, substantial inequity among property-owners, a reduction of investment in buildings, and, no doubt, to some corruption.

COMPLIANCE AND COLLECTION COSTS

Since the compliance costs to the taxpayers and the collection costs to the government add nothing to the national output, resources should not be wasted on them. Our major taxes have fairly low compliance and collection costs today, a few per cent of total revenue at most. But there are exceptions. State taxes on corporation income, which furnish little revenue, force companies that do business in many states to maintain elaborate business records not needed for other business purposes. For example, the assistant treasurer of a well-known independent stove company reports that 4 employees (one-sixth of the total accounting department) were required to prepare some 282 separate state, county, and municipal tax returns. Their cost, plus purchased legal and accounting services, was $39,000 a year. The total taxes paid were only $74,000, so that the compliance cost to the company was over half the amount of the taxes. These costs could be cut if all states accepted a uniform system of returns and agreed on some simple formulas for allocating business income to each state.

ENFORCEABILITY

A good tax system does not impose taxes which are impossible to enforce. Even where voluntary compliance is the rule, the possibility of verifying tax payments must exist, otherwise the tax becomes an invitation to break the law. Some of the deductions permitted under the federal income tax lead to this kind of situation. Local taxes and charitable contributions can be deduced from income. But who keeps track of every penny of gasoline taxes [1] or every dollar he gives to the dozens of charity drives? Without

[1] To reduce this problem the Internal Revenue Service has issued general guidelines of the "normal" deductions for general sales taxes in different states, and requires people to produce some documentation if they claim larger amounts.

records, people make a crude estimate which the government cannot check. The result: a temptation to be more generous in estimating than in giving. In our advanced society a great many taxes can be enforced; but in underdeveloped countries, where there is less record-keeping and many people are illiterate, the possibilities of enforceable taxation are much more circumscribed.

ACCEPTABILITY

Most important is that the tax system should be acceptable to the public. It should be consistent with people's notions of fair play, and should not be too onerous as compared to what they get for their tax dollars.

A Fair Tax System: Criteria of Equity

What we mean by a fair tax system is not a question of technical economics but of personal philosophy. Nevertheless, some principles have been developed over the years, and provide a useful framework. These are the benefit principle and the principle of ability to pay. Most discussion and controversy about equity is conducted within that framework.

The *benefit principle* calls for a distribution of taxes in accordance with the benefits received from the expenditures on which the taxes are spent. People pay for the goods and services received in the private economy, so why not in the public sector? If taxation violates the benefit principle, then public services are used to subsidize their users, since the services are received at other people's expense.

The benefit principle is, in fact, applied to highway taxation, where road-building is paid for out of earmarked highway-user taxes, set aside in separate accounts from which they cannot be "diverted" to other purposes. To some extent, the principle is also applied in the social-security field, where the payroll taxes are earmarked for the reserves from which the benefit payments are made. Many local services, such as the construction of sewers and streets, are partly financed out of special assessments levied on the residents who will be served.

Although fairness is one of the basic ideas behind these applications of the benefit principle, this form of taxation also provides a substitute for the market test. After all, if the people who will benefit from expenditures are not willing to pay for them through their taxes, presumably they are not worth their cost and should not be undertaken.[2]

The benefit principle can be applied only where the beneficiaries can be clearly identified. This is not true of most public services. How is the benefit of national defense or of education to be divided among the population? Thus, at best, the principle can provide a partial solution to the problem of fairness in taxation.

The *ability-to-pay principle* is the other standard of fairness. Adam Smith, back in 1776, listed this as the first canon of taxation, and most people take it for granted that a fair tax system calls on the richer members of the community to pay more taxes than the poor.

Actually, the ability-to-pay principle has two separate parts. It states not only that the rich should pay more but also that those who are similarly situated (e.g., have the same income) should pay the same taxes. This second idea, that "equals be treated equally," is called *horizontal equity*, while the proper division of the tax burden among people of different ability to pay is called *vertical equity*.

Measures of Ability to Pay: The Choice of Tax Base

It is one thing to agree that taxes be levied acording to ability to pay, but another to agree on the measure of this ability. We usually think of income as the best measure of ability to pay, for it determines a person's total command over resources during a stated period, with the recipient free to dispose as he sees fit, to consume, or to add to his wealth. The late Henry Simons of the University of Chicago, perhaps the outstanding thinker on this problem, went even further. He argued that all taxes, whatever their nominal base, ought to be considered to fall on individual incomes. When all the shifting is done, every tax is paid by somebody, and does, in fact, reduce that individual's

---

[2] This test of value is rather crude, since total revenues are compared with total cost, and no tests are performed at the margin.

income. Simons wanted to create a tax system with perfect horizontal equity in which the people with the same incomes would pay the same taxes, and with vertical equity also income-based. This ideal tax system would have required getting rid of most of the taxes other than income taxes, but would have made the definition of income truly comprehensive, including gifts, inheritances, and transfer payments.

Wealth might also be considered an appropriate measure of ability to pay. While, in a sense, it would be double taxation to tax both income and wealth, since the wealth produces income (which is taxed), nevertheless the mere possession of wealth may yield satisfaction on its own. Historically, the U.S. has probably been as much concerned with concentration of wealth as of income. Our estate and gift taxes are a response to this concern.

Recently another approach has received attention. Nicholas Kaldor of Cambridge, England, has advocated what he calls an expenditure tax, a tax on consumption. He argues that consumption rather than income should be the proper base of taxation. It is consumption which measures the resources which an individual actually withdraws from the economy for his personal use. The part of his income not consumed, his saving, adds to the country's capital stock and serves to raise total productive capacity; if an individual chooses to consume more than his income (by buying on credit or drawing on his past savings) he should pay a higher tax, since he is depleting the capital stock of the country. This idea is particularly attractive in under-developed countries where high consumption levels of the richer classes may make private capital accumulation small. An expenditure tax would discourage consumption by taxing it heavily, and encourage saving by granting it tax exemption. Such a tax could be progressive, with the rates rising with the total amount spent by an individual on consumption.[3]

In actual practice, governments use a great variety of tax bases. Personal and corporate income are the most important tax bases at our federal level; state and local governments rely more heavily on property, sales, and excise taxes. The variety of tax bases is a result of governments' perennial need for more money. When expenditures increase more than the revenue produced by the tax system, governments look for new sources, which usually means new tax bases. It has also been argued that excessive reliance on any one base produces adverse economic effects. Therefore, a tax system may do less economic damage if it raises moderate amounts from many bases rather than large amounts from a few.

Vertical Equity: The Structure of Tax Rates

Adam Smith argued that taxes should be *proportional* to income—that is, that everybody should pay the same percentage of his income as taxes. Today, we have gone one step further. We favor *progressive* taxes, which

---

[3] But think of the administrative problems. Every taxpayer would need to have records of his consumption expenditures, or else of his total income and the change in his wealth. Kaldor favors the second method. He would require taxpayers to submit both a balance sheet and an income statement as part of their tax return. Net additions on the balance sheet would reflect savings. The tax would be levied on income minus the net additions to wealth, which should correspond to consumption if the accounting is done precisely. Because of the administrative difficulties, the tax has been introduced in only two countries, India and Ceylon, and they seem to be about to give them up.

means that the fraction of income paid increases as income rises, so that the increase in tax payments is more than proportionate. This is the opposite of a *regressive* tax, under which the fraction of income paid declines as income rises.

Our tax system today is a mixture of all three kinds of taxes. The personal income tax is progressive, of course, with a tax rate of zero on the first $600 of income and a rate structure rising all the way to 91 per cent at the time of writing (1963), to be lowered to 70 per cent in 1965 under the tax program now being considered. But many other taxes are regressive, such as the heavy excises on gasoline, tobacco, and liquor. Take the tax on cigarettes, for example. A person with a high income is not going to smoke much more than a poor man, and even if he finds an expensive, exotic brand, the tax will be no greater since it is levied not on value but on the physical quantity. We also have some proportionate taxes. State sales taxes, particularly where they exempt food, are just about proportionate. Property taxes, which are still much the most important tax at the state and local level, range from regressive to proportionate. So are the federal excises on "luxuries"; they are levied on such broad categories as toiletries, appliances, leather goods, and so on, so that, in fact, they tax goods bought by everybody.

Taking the American tax system as a whole, is it progressive or regressive? This question is difficult to answer, because we not only have to know the composition of the tax system, but we also have to make some assumptions about the final incidence of each tax—i.e., to what extent the taxes are shifted and to whom. Professor Musgrave of Princeton has prepared some careful estimates of the total incidence of our tax system, using what seemed to him the most reasonable incidence assumptions about each tax. His

FIG. 5 Burden of the U.S. tax system by income class, 1954. (*Source:* R. A. Musgrave, "The Incidence of the Tax Structure and Its Effects on Consumption," in *Federal Tax Policy for Economic Growth and Stability*, Joint Economic Committee, 1955, p. 98.)

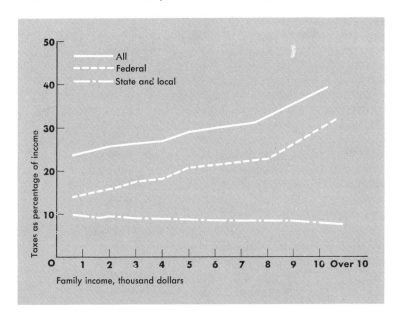

estimates are shown in Fig. 5.[4] You will notice that there is rather little progression from the low incomes through the middle-income range. Up to that point, the regressive excise and property taxes offset the progressive income taxes. In the upper incomes, the income tax becomes more important, to the point where it makes the entire tax structure progressive. As you would expect, the state and local tax systems, with their heavy reliance on sales, excise, and property taxes, are slightly regressive all the way up the income scale.

The Federal Personal Income Tax

We rely on the progressive federal income tax to assure a fair distribution of the tax burden. In fact, it is perhaps our main policy instrument for moderating the inequality of the distribution of income in our society. Table 9 shows its impact. So let us take a closer look at this tax.

The tax is levied on "all income, from whatever source derived," according to the Internal Revenue Code, but there are some important exceptions called *exclusions*. Government transfer payments (social security, unemployment and relief benefits), gifts and inheritances, and most incomes in kind (the benefit of home-ownership, on-the-farm food consumption) are not included in the legal income concept, called *adjusted gross income*. On the other hand, the legal definition includes much of the necessary cost of earning a living, such as commuting, lunch money, and the cost of dressing appropriately for the job, even though some of these items may reduce the income available for family consumption or saving.

TABLE 9

Distribution of Family Personal Income
Before and After Federal Income Tax, 1961

Quintiles (20 per cent groupings)	Average Income Before Tax	Tax	Average Income After Tax	Percentage Distribution Income Before Tax	Tax	Income After Tax
Lowest	$ 1,603	$ 57	$ 1,546	4.6	1.6	5.0
Second	3,805	223	3,583	11.0	6.3	11.5
Third	5,665	429	5,236	16.4	12.2	16.9
Fourth	7,329	671	7,158	22.6	19.0	23.0
Highest	15,678	2,147	13,531	45.4	60.9	43.6
				100.00	100.0	100.0
Top 5%	27,050	5,105	21,946	19.6	36.2	17.7

Source: U.S. Department of Commerce, *Survey of Current Business* (April, 1962), p. 18.

Our tax system recognizes that income alone is not the only factor in economic welfare. It therefore permits *deductions* of numerous items from adjusted gross income. The most important of these are:

[4] The Tax Foundation, Inc., has done a study for 1958, and found similar results. *Allocation of the Tax Burden by Income Class,* Project Note, No. 45, New York, 1960.

1. Taxes paid to local governments
2. Interest payments
3. Medical expenses above 3 per cent of income
4. Contributions to charity
5. Casualty losses, such as losses from fire and theft not compensated by insurance.

If the taxpayer chooses not to claim itemized deductions, he can claim a *standard deduction* of 10 per cent of his income, up to $500 per person. (The current tax proposals would allow a minimum standard deduction of $300 for a single person plus $100 for each dependent.)

In addition, the law permits *exemptions,* $600 for the taxpayer and for each of his dependents, plus an extra exemption for people over 65 and the

FIG. 6   Nominal rate structure for married couples, federal income tax, 1963, and for 1965 under president's proposed program.

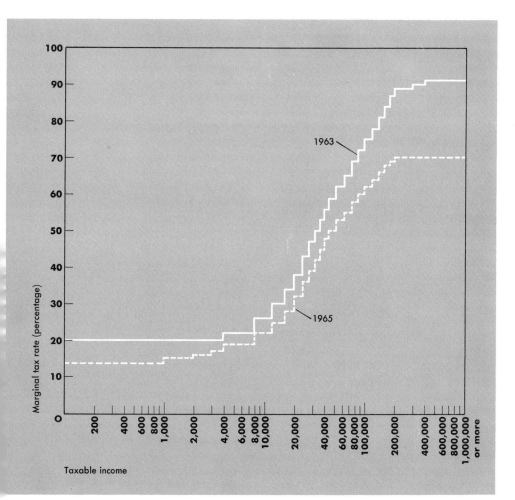

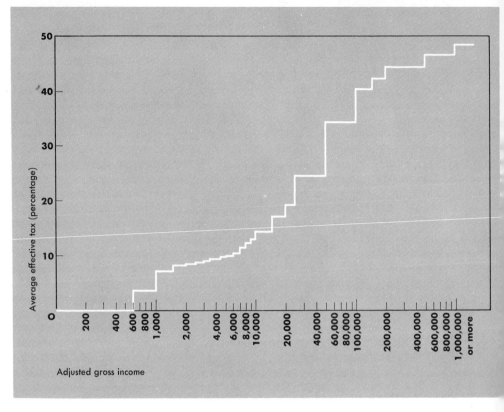

FIG. 7 Average effective tax rates. (*Source:* U.S. Treasury, Statistics of Income, 1960, Individual Income Tax Returns, p. 65.)

blind. The exemption is related to the bare cost of subsistence, an amount therefore left immune from taxation.[5]

Ever since World War II, the rate structure has been highly progressive, with a maximum rate in excess of 90 per cent in effect most of the time. This extreme progression was adopted at the beginning of World War II in order to take the profit out of war, at a time when there was even consideration of an absolute income ceiling of $25,000 that anyone could keep after taxes. These rates were more extreme than the American people really wanted; the spirit of egalitarianism is not that strong in the United States. In fact, there have been enough loopholes in the tax structure to keep actual rates lower than the rather frightening Fig. 6 suggests. (The figure also shows the rate structure that would result from enactment of the current tax program). The average effective tax rates—that is, the actual tax paid divided by

[5] The law also permits some *tax credits,* specific reductions of tax liability. So far this has been a minor device in the United States, the only significant cases being (1) a credit equal to 4 per cent of the taxpayer's dividends; (2) a retirement income credit, a complicated provision designed to give equal treatment to retired persons living on pensions but not receiving tax-exempt social-security benefits; (3) credits against foreign income taxes; and (4) the investment credit, discussed in Chapter 6. The tax credit device has received increased attention in recent years because it offers the possibility of giving the same absolute amount of tax relief throughout the income scale, independent of the rate structure. Thus, the President's tax reform proposals of 1963 called for a $300 tax credit for persons over age 65 to replace a host of special provisions for this group, an amount that would be the same for anyone with sufficient income to have $300 of tax liability, whether it is $5,000 or a million. The Congress did not accept this proposal.

adjusted gross income, are shown in Fig. 7. In no income bracket do they reach 50 per cent, even when income exceeds $1 million.[6]

Issues of Fairness

Observers have pointed out that so many exclusions, exemptions, and deductions have crept into the tax system that the tax base has shrunk to a point where it is only three-sevenths of personal income. Table 10 summarizes this phenomenon for the year 1960. If the tax base were not so narrow, the rate structure could be lower. For example, if we could increase the base by a quarter, we could lower the rates by a fifth and still obtain the same revenue. In the sense that the numerous special provisions have narrowed the tax base and forced us to retain higher rates to raise the necessary revenues, they have been self-defeating.

[6] Even that chart overstates the low rates paid on income because the income concept used leaves out one-half of capital gains, interest from tax-exempt securities and the exclusions listed above. If all of capital gains were included in income, the peak rate paid by any income class would be less than 40 per cent.

TABLE 10

Erosion of the Tax Base, 1960 (Billions of dollars)

Personal Income (National Income Accounts)		400.8
—**Exclusions** from personal income		85.5
—Transfer payments	28.7	
—Supplements to wages and salaries (fringe benefits)	10.3	
—Income in kind (home-ownership) and unreported income	21.9	
—Miscellaneous, (some military pay, sick pay, $50 of dividends, tax-exempt interest, etc.)	8.9	
—Non-reported income	33.4	
+Employee contributions to social security	9.2	
+Miscellaneous (taxed half of capital gains, etc.)	8.5	
Adjusted Gross Income on tax returns (including 18.3 on non-taxable returns)		315.5
—**Deductions**		48.3
—Standard deduction (10% of Adjusted Gross Income up to $1000 for couple)	13.0	
—Itemized deductions	35.3	
—State and local taxes	10.5	
—Interest paid	8.4	
—Contributions	6.8	
—Medical and dental	5.2	
—Other	4.4	
—**Exemptions** (excludes exemptions in excess of net income on non-taxable returns)		95.7
Ordinary ($600 per person)	92.0	
Extraordinary for aged and blind	3.7	
=**Taxable Income**		171.5
Total tax before credits		39.9
—Tax credits (dividends, retirement income, etc.)		0.5
=**Tax**		39.4

Base-broadening reform is difficult to enact because every one of the exclusions, deductions, and exemptions was put into the tax law for a specific purpose, to relieve some particular inequity or to respond to some particular pressure. Thus, a rehabilitation of the tax base requires reversing previous successful campaigns by various groups to get preferential treatment. Those same groups defend their privileges. You may want to go through the list yourself and decide in your own mind which exclusions, deductions, exemptions, and credits you believe to be just.

DOES INCOME-SPLITTING PENALIZE BACHELORS?

Since 1948 the law has allowed married couples to use "income-splitting"—that is, to attribute half the couple's income to the husband and half to the wife, regardless of who earned it. With a progressive tax structure, this reduces the total tax payment in all cases above the lowest bracket, since it shifts income from the top bracket of the person with the larger income, usually the husband, to the lower bracket of the other. Bachelors do not receive the benefit of this provision, of course, and it makes quite a difference, as you can see from Table 11.

TABLE 11

**Income Taxation of Bachelors, Married Couples,
and Heads of Households (1963 rates)**

Taxable Income	Tax Liability		
	Bachelor	Married Couple	Head of Household
$ 2,000	$ 400	$ 400	$ 400
6,000	1,360	1,240	1,300
10,000	2,640	2,200	2,420
20,000	7,260	5,280	6,260
50,000	26,820	20,300	23,580
100,000	67,320	53,640	60,480

While Congress has not been sympathetic to the plight of bachelors, it did feel that it was unfair to widowers and divorced persons raising children. To put them into a more similar position with married couples, it allowed a special set of tax rates for "heads of households," which gives them one-half of the benefit of income-splitting.

IS THE TAX SYSTEM TOO GENEROUS TO HOME-OWNERS?

The system of deductions is particularly favorable to home-ownership. Two of the biggest expenses of owning a house are the payment of local taxes and interest on the mortgage, both of which are deductible; other fields of consumption do not offer comparable tax savings. Capital invested in a home earns a tax-free return, since we do not tax the income-in-kind stemming from the use of the home. In contrast, a renter, who puts his capital into securities, pays taxes on the income and pays his rent out of after-tax income.

But there are social and political considerations to be weighed also. We really like to encourage home-ownership; it is said to make people more stable and secure, reduce juvenile delinquency, and so on. Also, the deduction of local taxes from the federal tax base is a long-established principle of our multi-level system of government. Without this deduction, opposition to local taxes would be greater, and local services, particularly education, would suffer. Thus, this deduction takes some of the sting out of the local tax burdens and helps the financial position of states and localities.

THE SPECIAL TREATMENT OF CAPITAL GAINS

If a person makes money in the stock market or realizes other gains from having his capital assets become more valuable, he will not be taxed at the regular personal income tax rates, provided he has held the asset at least 6 months. Instead, he pays only one-half the tax, up to a maximum rate of 25 per cent. Thus, even an individual who pays a 91 per cent rate on ordinary income never pays more than 25 per cent on a long-term gain.[7] This is obviously a very powerful tax provision. At the top of the income scale (at 1963 rates), it means the difference between keeping 9 cents out of a dollar of ordinary income and keeping 75 cents out of a dollar of capital gain.[8]

As this gap between capital gains rates and ordinary income rates has continued, businesses and individuals have used it as a method of tax avoidance. For example, stock options have come into widespread use as a means of paying top-level executives. Here is how it works:

> The company gives Vice President *A* the option to purchase a thousand shares of its common stock at a price of $35, an option which he can exercise any time, say, during 3 years. Suppose the stock rises to $45; *A* exercises the option, buys the thousand shares at $35, holds them for a few years during which time the price of stock stays constant, and then sells it. He has made $10,000, which is a capital gain, taxable at a maximum rate of 25 per cent.

The stock option was originally used in order to give professional managers an ownership stake in the business, to make their interests coincide with those of the stockholders. But under the pressure of the tax laws, more and more stock options are given to executives as a form of income subject to favorable tax treatment.

Capital gains have been used in other ways to furnish relief from the regular rates. The sale of timber, livestock, and some mineral rights is accorded capital gains treatment. So is the sale of a patent, an incentive to inventors. Where a man has built up a highly prosperous business, perhaps through a successful new product, he may be unable, because of the progressive income tax, to pass on the benefits to his family except by selling out. Our

[7] The President's tax program would ease the taxation of capital gains further. On assets held 2 years, only 40 per cent of the usual rate would be applied, with an absolute limit of 21 per cent.

[8] The tax can be escaped altogether as long as the asset is not sold. Only capital gains "realized" in a market transaction are subject to tax. It has been estimated that over half of all capital gains are never realized during people's lifetimes. Upon the transfer of the asset at death, assets are revalued, and any gains achieved up to that date cease to be subject to tax.

history is replete with cases where the entrepreneur sells out to a larger company, converting the value he has created by his innovation into a capital gain.

The present system has some questionable economic characteristics. It penalizes earned income, such as wages and salaries, while giving a tax break to incomes which qualify as capital gains. It also has the effect of making corporation stockholders more anxious to have stock appreciate in value rather than to yield dividends. This has encouraged major corporations to retain their earnings and rely on internal funds for investment rather than to compete for funds in the open capital market. Most fundamentally, the capital gains provisions make a mockery of the regular rate structure as people figure out more and more ways to take their income in this form.

Why do we give such favorable treatment to capital gains? I believe there are five reasons: (1) People do not seem to consider capital gains exactly like other income. They are "paper profits" which people frequently put back into other securities, rather than include in their regular household budgets. People separate their thinking about capital and about income, and even though an increase in the value of a person's wealth is income under most reasonable definitions, people may nevertheless think of it as a part of their capital accounts, as something to be reinvested rather than consumed. (2) A well-functioning capitalist system requires that not all accumulation take place inside corporations. Individuals should also be able to accumulate capital and make it available in an open market, where new and expanding firms can compete for it. Under the full progressive income tax rates, it would become very difficult for substantial amounts of capital to accumulate in private hands. Thus we sacrifice some fairness in the tax system to maintain a healthy system of private capital accumulation. (3) Capital gains are the rewards for successful risk-taking. We do not allow unlimited deductions for losses, so some favorable tax treatment for gains is justified to keep investment from becoming a "Heads you win, tails I lose" proposition. (4) The capital gains rates act as a safety valve for the progressive tax system. By giving people the chance to accumulate a fraction of their income at the more favorable capital gains rates, we make the progressive rate structure more acceptable when applied to the rest of their income. (5) Capital gains frequently come in large chunks, when a substantial asset is sold. Unless there were a special tax treatment for capital gains, the workings of the progressive rate structure would push the individual into a very high tax bracket for the year that he realized his gain.

TAX SHELTERS

A tax shelter is a device which permits the taxpayer to plow back earnings on capital without their being subject to tax, at least until such time as he removes the capital for his personal use. Because of our desire to facilitate capital accumulation, we have allowed, perhaps even encouraged, the widespread use of tax shelters.

Company pension plans are a prime example. The money paid into a pension plan by a company is not considered income to the employee until he has retired and the pension is being paid out. Thus, the capital can accumulate inside the pension fund over the working life of the employee without being taxed. Furthermore, a person's income after retirement is likely to be less than it was during his working years, so the rate at which the pension will be taxed will presumably be lower.[9]

The self-employed, such as lawyers, doctors, and owners of small businesses, cannot participate in these company pension plans, and therefore find it more difficult to accumulate wealth to provide for their retirement years. On the one hand, it is only fair to provide them with the same opportunities that corporations employees enjoy under the tax laws. On the other hand, this is a perfect example of eroding tax base. What starts as the preferential treatment of one group becomes extended to other groups who claim that they are entitled to the same privilege. In 1962, after years of discussion, Congress gave the self-employed the privilege of setting up their own pension plans with tax shelter privileges, though only for limited amounts and hedged by numerous restrictions.

Life insurance is another important tax shelter. The reserves built up by each policy are allowed to earn interest without being taxed to the individual until such time as the policy is paid off. If the policy pays off at death, it permanently escapes income taxation.

TAX-EXEMPT SECURITIES

The interest on the bonds of state and local governments has traditionally been exempt from federal income taxation. As a result, individuals in very high tax brackets can purchase these securities to earn a tax-free income. The bonds consequently have been bid up in price, although a good quality local bond yields less than a U.S. government bond. This has greatly facilitated the debt-financing of the rapidly rising state and local expenditures.

In earlier years, the interest yield on the bonds was bid so low that this loophole had little value. No tax was paid but not much income was collected. But as the volume of local debt has kept on increasing by leaps and bounds, the premium on the bonds has shrunk, so that today many of the tax-free bonds yield interest of 4 per cent or more. Thus the benefit to the localities is smaller, while the benefit to the purchasers grows. No serious effort has been made in recent years to close this loophole, because local governments wish to retain this marketing aid for their bonds.

THE PROBLEM OF UNEVEN INCOMES

People whose incomes are bunched into a small part of their working life, such as professional athletes, entertainers, and authors of best-sellers, are treated harshly by the tax law. In the brief years in which they earn their large incomes they are subject to the highly progressive tax rates. Were they to earn the same amount of money in a more even pattern, they would pay substantially less tax. A ballplayer who earns a modest income for a few years, then becomes a major league star, earning perhaps $50,000 a year, and reverts to his modest income when his playing days are over, may pay in taxes almost half of what he earned during his best years. Someone else, receiving the same total revenue, but in the more typical gradually rising lifetime pattern, will pay much less.

It has long been proposed that people in these categories be allowed

9 There are many rules about organizing pension plans before they can be eligible for favorable tax treatment. For example, the pension plan must be open to all employees at least in principle, not to just a few top executives.

to "average" their incomes. This would enable them to compute their tax liability as if the income were earned, not in one year, but spread evenly over many years. As in other matters, people have learned to live with the system and have figured out devices which permit them to engage in substitutes for averaging. These include deferred payment contracts in which one year's compensation is paid out over longer intervals, sometimes not until retirement. In the case of movie stars, the tax laws have pushed them into organizing their own producing companies, so that they can take their earnings in ways other than straight salaries.

To reduce the worst cases of inequity, the beginning of averaging was included in the tax reforms of 1963. If one year's income exceeds the average of the previous 4 years both by more than a third and also by a minimum of $3,000, the progression of the tax rates to be applied to that excess is considerably reduced below normal.

FAIRNESS IN OTHER TAXES

Although most of the controversy about fairness centers on the personal income tax, the other types of taxes also raise some equity questions. I mention only a few common types of issues.

Estate and gift taxes. The U.S. has highly progressive estate and gift taxes. The first $60,000 of an estate are exempt. The rates start at 3 per cent, reach 18 per cent at $100,000, 39 per cent at $1 million, and 77 per cent at $10 million.[11] Even more than in the case of the income tax, there are numerous means of avoiding the tax. The legal provisions are extremely complicated, and the impact of the tax on an estate is capricious, depending partly on the amount of effort and legal skill which has gone into the planning of an estate. Estate taxes were levied not just because wealth is a measure of ability to pay but also to prevent the concentration of wealth in a few hands. The present taxes are rather ineffective in promoting these objectives.

No major reform effort has been made, first because the law is so complex that it is far from clear what could be done. More important, the taxes probably fall heavily on capital, not on consumption, since people do not appear to save more during their lifetime merely to leave the same after-tax estate. Thus the tax must fall on the estate and its beneficiaries, and to the extent that they would not consume their inheritance the tax must come out of capital. With economic growth a major policy objective, we have shown little inclination to increase the taxation of capital.

Discriminatory excise taxes. Our system of excise taxes applies only to certain commodities, leaving others untaxed. The chief complaint about these taxes does not come from consumers but from the producers of the taxed commodities, both companies and workers. They feel that their sales are penalized and hence profits and employment are reduced, that they are discriminated against as an industry compared to other industries. For example, until 1960 nightclub bills were taxed 20 per cent, presumably because Congress frowned on lavish expense account living. This was the only 20 per cent luxury tax then on the books. But what is a nightclub? A restaurant with live entertainment, including a lone piano player or a small band. Result: The tax led to unemployment among musicians as the smaller

[11] Gift tax rates are 75 per cent of the estate rates and are mainly designed to prevent escape from the estate tax.

places put in canned music in order not to have to charge their customers the 20 per cent tax. Musicians and club-owners pleaded for relief from the tax, and it was cut to 10 per cent.

PREFERENTIAL TREATMENT FOR SOME INDUSTRIES
UNDER THE CORPORATION INCOME TAX

While most industries pay the full 52 per cent of their profits as federal corporation income tax, a few receive preferential treatment. The natural-resource industries, particularly crude-oil producers, pay lower rates because of the *depletion allowance*. On the theory that the sale of minerals is not like the sale of the output of an ordinary business but rather involves the sale of a company's assets, the Congress, back in 1913, allowed these industries to deduct a small percentage of their total revenue from their taxable income as a depletion allowance. Over the years, this percentage has been increased, and similar allowances have been extended to other minerals, including coal and most other mined products—even to such "minerals" as sand, gravel, and oyster shells. More than half of the $1.5 billion of tax saving accrues to oil production, however.

These provisions have made the oil industry particularly attractive for investment by people in high personal income tax brackets. For example, a movie star who sees himself about to land in the 91 per cent bracket can take part of his income and invest it in oil wells. If he strikes oil, the resultant income is taxable at a low rate because of the depletion allowance. If he misses a strike, he has only lost 9-cent dollars; the government would have received the other 91 cents anyway.

The depletion allowance has produced a distortion in investment decisions. Too much capital is attracted to the oil industry. As a result, the rate of return on oil has been driven down to the point where the after-tax return is no greater than the economy average. There is also much excess capacity.

In recent years the depletion allowance has usually been justified in terms of the riskiness of this form of investment. Only 1 well drilled out of 9 exploratory attempts produces enough oil to make it worth developing, though more than half of all production wells prove successful. The favorable tax treatment, it has been argued, is necessary to encourage people to enter this very risky field.

Other companies also enjoy partial or complete exemption from the corporate income tax. Life insurance companies receive a different tax treatment because of the difficulty in defining their income, given the necessity of setting aside reserves against future claims. Cooperatives, savings and loan associations, and mutual savings banks receive favorable treatment because they are not corporations and have some of the characteristics of non-profit institutions. Where they compete with similar institutions organized as corporations, they have a great advantage and can undersell those who pay the full tax, and in some cases, have driven them out of business.

The Double Taxation Issue

It has struck many people as unfair that we should levy both a personal and a corporation income tax, because it means that the same income is taxed twice. Suppose that a corporation produces an income of a million dollars. It will pay a corporation income tax of about one-half. Suppose now that it pays the remaining half million dollars to its stockholders and that they pay an average tax rate of 60 per cent on these dividends. Taking both taxes together, this means that out of the million dollars of income, the government collects a total of $800,000, leaving only $200,000 to the stockholders. If the money were earned by a partnership, the corporation income tax would not be paid at all; 50 per cent seems like a stiff price to pay for the privilege of incorporating.

In 1954 a first step was taken to give relief by enacting a dividend exclusion and a dividend credit. The exclusion permitted every taxpayer to exclude the first $50 of dividends from his taxable income ($100 for joint returns); the credit permitted him to deduct 4 per cent of his dividends from his tax. The theory is that the corporation income tax is a form of withholding of the personal income tax on dividend income. A lower rate should then be subsequently applied when the personal tax is computed.

These measures were thought to be first steps toward a more complete integration of the corporation and personal taxes into one comprehensive income tax. One might have envisaged that ultimately the entire corporation income tax on distributed profits would be considered withholding on the personal tax (which would entitle some people to refunds). A tax would still have to be levied on the part of profits retained by the corporation to keep it from escaping taxation altogether.

However, no further steps were taken. President Kennedy repeatedly asked for repeal of the steps taken, and the House of Representatives voted to repeal the dividend credit in 1963 (but doubled the exclusion).

Why has the double taxation theory not carried the day? First, the corporation income tax is probably shifted in part, and to that extent one cannot speak of double taxation of stockholders, since the burden is borne by consumers. Second, some people consider the corporation income tax a "doing business tax"—that is, a tax based on the benefit principle, a payment for the privilege of operating an enterprise within the framework of our economy. On that theory, all businesses, including partnerships and cooperatives, would be proper subjects of the tax; in fact, the government has attempted in recent years to tax more heavily some of the larger non-corporate enterprises, such as mutual savings banks, savings and loan associations, and cooperatives, even if they do not adopt the conventional corporate form of organization. Third, some observers refuse to treat the corporation and its stockholders as synonymous. The double taxation theory views the corporation as no more than a legal intermediary between the stockholder and the income-creating production process. If it is considered an independent institution, a social organism with a structure of its own, with its own purposes and motivations, then it may be an entity properly subject to taxation. Finally, and this may be the most important reason for the continued use of the corporation income tax, it is an excellent revenue-raiser. Implicit in any scheme to lighten the total tax load so drastically is the necessity to find revenue substitutes, and it is very difficult to think of alternatives that would produce the $25 to $30 billion that we now collect from this source.

Summary

The American tax system succeeds in raising an enormous amount of money to finance the government's activities at home and abroad. A tax system of such magnitude must be designed to minimize any negative impact on the performance of the economy.

The tax system must have certain administrative qualities, including certainty, low compliance and collection costs, enforceability, and acceptability.

The system must also be fair, both to promote the objective of an equitable distribution of income and to assure continued voluntary compliance by taxpayers. Two principles of equity have been advanced—the benefit principle, which has only limited applicability, and the ability-to-pay principle. Under the benefit principle, taxes are levied according to the benefit people receive from the expenditures for which the taxes are spent. Ability-to-pay involves questions of horizontal equity, of treating equals equally; and of vertical equity, the distribution of tax burdens among people with different abilities-to-pay.

Income is most commonly considered the best measure of ability-to-pay, although wealth and consumption expenditures have also been discussed. Taxes can be regressive, proportionate or progressive, depending upon their relative burden on different income classes. Many of the issues of fairness relate to the federal personal income tax, our major policy instrument for changing the distribution of income. These issues relate to the use of the various exclusions, exemptions, and deductions under the tax. Their wide use under various special provisions of the tax law has led to an erosion of the tax base, with less than half of all personal income proving to be taxable. This erosion has led to higher tax rates to meet the financial needs of the government.

Other issues of fairness relate to the system of excise taxes which are thought to penalize some industries, and to the especially favorable treatment given to some industries and some forms of business organization under the corporation income tax. It has also been questioned whether it is fair to tax income from corporate business "twice," first as corporation income, and then once more as individual dividend income.

6

TAXES, EFFICIENCY, AND GROWTH

The preceding chapter dealt with the relation of the tax system to the achievement of a fair distribution of income, and more specifically, a fair distribution of the tax burden. This chapter discusses the effects of the tax system on two other long-term objectives, efficiency and growth. In the succeeding chapter we turn to the short-term objective of economic stability.

The Tax System and the Efficiency of the Economy

Neutrality has long been considered one of the virtues of a good tax system. By this we mean that private production and consumption decisions are not affected, that the allocation of resources in the private sector remains undisturbed.

A tax system as pervasive as ours cannot be neutral. People do take tax considerations into account in their personal and business decisions. An employee may decide not to bother with overtime because the taxes will take a quarter of the additional pay; a businessman may pass up the opportunity to make an investment because the prospective return after taxes is not worth the risk; a housewife may buy commodity *B* rather than *A* because *A* is subject to an excise tax and *B* is not. Perhaps someone may even smoke or drink a little less just because of the very high taxes on tobacco and alcohol.

Sometimes the government favors a departure from neutrality, as in the case of liquor and tobacco. But usually, the influence on decision-making is incidental to the government's need to raise revenue. The resultant deviations from neutrality must be considered distortions in decision-making.

These distortions are a serious matter in a market economy. We rely on consumers' expression of their preferences in the market to influence businesses in their production decisions. To show how taxes can distort this market mechanism, here is a simple example:

Suppose that consumers have been buying certain quantities of commodities *A* and *B* and that the price of *A* is $3 and the price of *B* is $3; these are equilibrium prices which reflect the relative attractiveness of the two commodities to consumers and the relative costs to producers. Now suppose a tax of 30 cents is placed on *A,* and the price, including tax, goes up to $3.20, the producers absorbing the remaining 10 cents of the tax. Consumers will normally buy less of *A* because it is priced higher in relation to *B* than before. Producers will also change their output; the price that they receive for *A* is now only $2.90. Because of the tax, less of *A* is produced relative to *B*.

Assuming fully employed resources, the total goods available to the private economy have to fall if the government spends the tax revenues to purchase resources for its own use. This is unavoidable, since the tax system releases the resources to be absorbed by the public sector. But in the example, there is an additional loss to the private economy. The price of *A* is no longer a sound signaling device which businesses can use to find out the value of *A* to consumers. The two sides of the market no longer operate by the same price. Consumers consider the price with tax, producers the price without tax. The tax has driven a wedge into the price system. As a result, the private economy is misled into producing the wrong combination of goods, underproducing those heavily taxed. Thus the resources are no longer used in an optimal way. This additional loss, beyond the value of resources withdrawn from private use through the tax, is called the "deadweight loss of taxation" because this loss has no offsetting gain to the government. It is simply the loss suffered from the reduction in the efficiency of the economy, a cost of having an imperfect tax system.[1]

From the point of view of having an efficient allocation of resources in the economy, it is desirable to have a tax system which causes as little dead-weight tax loss as possible. This is accomplished by levying taxes in such a way that decision-making is not affected—that is to say, that the tax cannot be avoided by adjusting behavior. The extreme form of such a tax is a head tax, a lump-sum tax imposed on living persons. Because the amount to be paid has to be the same for everybody, it has to be set low so that it can be borne by low-income people; hence not much money can be raised by this method. No other tax is completely unavoidable. Excise taxes can be avoided by buying less of the taxed commodities; income taxes can be avoided by working less and earning less income; property taxes can be avoided by holding less property, and so on.

There are two general rules for keeping the deadweight loss at a minimum while raising any given amount of revenue. First, only those things should be taxed which generate slight adjustments in behavior. In the case of excise taxation, this means that more revenue should be raised from those items for which the demand and supply are inelastic. Governments discovered early that commodities with inelastic demands made convenient bases for taxation. In the Middle Ages, the salt tax was used widely. People needed salt for their diet; there was no substitute. Hence salt had an inelastic demand. Today, gasoline, liquor, and tobacco seem to play the same role. Thus it turns out that governments' desire for productive revenue sources tends to coincide with the economic principle that the deadweight tax loss be kept to a minimum. Unfortunately, the principle of minimizing deadweight tax loss often runs counter to the equity objective. Items in inelastic demand

---

[1] This argument can be illustrated by a diagram.

Let S and D be the supply and demand curves for a product without tax. At price b, a units are sold. Now suppose a tax of t per unit sold is imposed. As seen by the consumers, the supply curve now includes the tax, and becomes S'. Consumers buy less, a', at a higher price, d. Producers sell less, but receive a lower price (net of tax), equal to e. With the supply curves reflecting marginal costs, producers' profits decline by the shaded area $bxfe$. With the demand curve reflecting marginal utilities of consumers, the loss of utility that they suffer from having to pay higher prices is equal to the shaded area $bxgd$ (this loss is called loss of consumers' surplus). The government collects tax revenues equal to the rectangle $efgd$, an amount equal to the tax rate times the number of units sold. Thus the government's gain is less than the total loss suffered by producers and consumers. This net loss is the deadweight loss.

This loss is due to the disruption of an efficient allocation of resources. Before the tax, marginal cost equaled marginal utility at the point where the supply and demand curves met. The tax destroys the marginal efficiency condition, with marginal utility now exceeding marginal cost. The analysis assumes that an efficient situation prevailed before the tax was imposed.

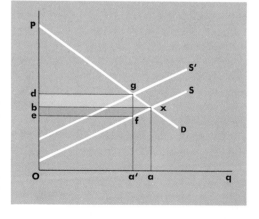

tend to be necessities, like bread, which loom particularly large in the budgets of low-income families.

The second rule for minimizing the deadweight tax loss is to maintain high average rates of taxation but low marginal rates. The deadweight tax loss originates in the induced changes of private decisions, changes made at the margin, and hence depends on the marginal tax rates. On the other hand, average rates determine the total revenue. Thus, a tax causes less deadweight tax loss per dollar of revenue if its average rate is high but the marginal rate is low. Many of our taxes, such as excise taxes and most property taxes, are proportionate, making marginal and average rates the same. But our personal income tax has the opposite characteristic, with marginal rates much higher than average rates, so the incentive to change decisions is very strong in relation to the total revenue which is raised. The conflict between equity and efficiency is particularly acute in this case.

Progressive Income Taxes and the Supply of Effort

The single most important question about the effect of the U.S. income tax system on the economy's efficiency is the impact of the high marginal tax rates on people's willingness to put forth their best productive efforts. If a man has to turn over, say, one-half of his income from additional work, perhaps a lawyer working weekends, a doctor taking on additional patients, or a salesman making night-time calls, he will certainly have less incentive than if he were able to keep everything he makes. No one can doubt that these effects are pertinent; the question is: How widespread and how important are they? For if the high rates have diminished effort substantially throughout the economy, we are giving up a lot of economic performance for the sake of equity.

Two major studies have been conducted on this question. Professor Sanders of the Harvard Business School interviewed 160 corporate executives.[2] These were his major findings. The typical executive has to put forth his best efforts, taxes or no, to fulfill the requirements of his job and to progress on the promotional ladder of his company. Furthermore, executives are not motivated by income alone; equally important is the desire to do a good job, to be favorably recognized by fellow executives, and to know the excitement that comes from conducting a business successfully. While salary is very important as an indicator of the place of the executive in the hierarchy of the company and as a symbol of achievement, it is the relative salary compared to others which is important in this regard. Since everyone pays taxes, the symbolic value of salary is undiminished. Furthermore, the companies adapt their method of payment to executives to reduce tax liability, through stock options, pension plans, and other devices.

But in certain areas, the negative effect of the tax system was very clear. The willingness of executives to move from one company to another, or from one location to another is definitely reduced, and this is especially true of upper-level executives over the age of 50. Typically, they have sizable stakes in the pension plans of their present company, which they would forfeit if they were to resign; it would be very difficult for another company to match

---

[2] T. H. Sanders, *Effects of Taxation on Executives*, Harvard Graduate School of Business Administration, Division of Research, 1951.

these accumulated pension rights. (The growth of the pension plans was partly a response to the progressive tax rates.) In the case of locational changes, a middle-aged family will have taken root in the community, have friends and a home to which they have become accustomed. To pull up stakes at this stage in life imposes psychic costs for which no moving allowance can compensate, yet the resultant increase in after-tax income can not be very great because of the progressive tax. The number of people in this position, upper-level executives asked to change jobs or locations, is not great but they are important. Our capitalist economy depends on the skill of top management. Competition for the top positions and for the top personnel —even across company lines—is necessary to put the right man into the right post. The tax system has clearly made this more difficult.

Professor Break of the University of California at Berkeley interviewed 306 lawyers and accountants in England.[3] This was an ideal group to study because top-income tax rates are even higher in England than in this country, and lawyers and accountants are independent professional men who control their own work effort; they can take on fewer clients, take longer vacations, or retire earlier. Break found that the men interviewed fell into three groups. (1) Forty men reported that taxes had a definite adverse effect on incentive, ranging from blanket refusal to accept additional work, to reduced effort in seeking new clients, to turning down work occasionally which was also unattractive for other reasons, such as excessive travel. (2) Thirty-one men complained that they had to work harder because of taxes. Some of them said that they were unable to retire when they wished because they had been unable to accumulate sufficient wealth. Others reported that they had to work harder day-by-day in order to realize an after-tax income sufficient to sustain the standard of living to which they were accustomed. The remaining 235 men reported minor or no effects on their work, although many grumbled quite a bit about taxes. Typically, they enjoyed their work, were happy to have a large and successful practice, and felt they owed it to their clients to do the best for them they could.

These studies deal only with very specialized groups of people. What about the general working population? Our evidence is extremely limited, but so far nothing suggests that unions have insisted on a shorter work week, that workers have refused to work overtime, or that fewer wives enter the labor force because of taxes.[4]

In summary, then, it appears that the adverse effect of personal income taxes on the supply of effort is probably slight. This is because people are not motivated by money income alone, because the extent of their control over their own working conditions is limited, and because the methods of payment by employers have been adapted to reduce the tax burden.

This brings us to what is perhaps the most important distortion caused by the tax system in our economy: the social waste of tax avoidance itself. According to our principles of law, a person has no obligation to pay more taxes than is legally required. The tax law clearly presents to all upper- and many middle-income taxpayers the means to reduce their tax burden signifi-

---

[3] G. F. Break, "Income Taxes and Incentives to Work: an Empirical Study," *American Economic Review,* Vol. XLVII, No. 5 (September, 1957), pp. 529-549.

[4] In England, however, where there is no income-splitting (the wife's income is added to the husband's and the total is taxed at one progressive rate schedule), the tax system raises greater obstacles to women joining the labor force.

cantly by rearranging their personal affairs. Seeking out capital gains rather than ordinary income on investments, organizing personal wealth into trusts, buying tax-exempt local bonds, taking income in the form of pensions, stock options, or deferred compensation contracts—these are all thoroughly legal and reputable means of avoiding taxes. As we have lived with our present tax system, people have learned to use these devices. Consequently, an immense amount of effort has gone into tax avoidance. Corporation executives who should be spending all their time thinking about the affairs of their companies are distracted into managing their personal investments so they will yield capital gains or other tax advantages. Family financial arrangements are set up not only from a personal but also from a tax point of view. For example, income and estate taxes are reduced if wealth is not left to children but is put in trust for a later generation, with only the income accruing to the children; as a result, the second generation never acquires the maturing responsibility of managing the family wealth. The job is turned over to professional trustees, banks, and lawyers, who manage the wealth conservatively and do not make the funds available for risky ventures.

The tax system has also created a whole profession of experts, of accountants and lawyers who advise people on their tax affairs. If our tax system were simpler, with lower rates and fewer loopholes, the high intellectual qualities of this group could be devoted to some other purpose. Finally, the ever-increasing tax-avoidance practices constitute a threat to the tax system itself. As taxpayer morale weakens, the tax base erodes, and tax rates need to be kept high to produce necessary revenues.

The Tax System and Economic Growth

As economic growth became an important national objective in recent years, the question was raised more and more insistently whether the tax system had a retarding effect. Several major tax changes have already been made to facilitate growth. The re-examination continues, and several far-reaching proposals are being debated.

THE CORPORATION INCOME TAX AND ECONOMIC GROWTH

Because the United States relies so heavily on giant corporations for her industrial capital formation, it is the corporation income tax which has to be given particular attention in dealing with the issue of taxes and growth. The tax affects (1) the incentive to invest—that is, the profit anticipated from an investment; (2) the riskiness of investments; and (3) the supply of investible funds.

The structure of the tax is simple. Its base is the net income of the corporation. The rate is a flat 52 per cent, except for the first $25,000 of income on which the rate is only 30 per cent.[5] There is no exemption.

The tax makes the government a partner in every corporation. If the tax is not shifted, government takes half of all profits and thereby lowers the expected net return on investment projects. Projects will be undertaken only if their expected return exceeds the cost of capital and compensates for the risk being taken. Inevitably, companies will invest less if the government receives half the gain in the event the investment proves successful.

[5] The current tax proposals would lower the rates to 47% and 22%.

There are some qualifications to this picture. First, while the government is a partner in the gains, to some extent it also is a partner in the losses. When a company suffers a loss on a project, it is permitted to subtract this loss from the profits it earns elsewhere, thus reducing its tax by one-half of the losses. Where a company has no profits from other activities against which to offset losses, it is free to "carry" the losses "forward" against the profits of the 5 following years, or it can carry them "backward" against profits in the 3 preceding years. These loss offsets are incomplete (1) because some companies never have any profits against which to offset losses, and (2) even if a project is clearly on the point of failing early, some of the losses cannot be written off more quickly than the fixed capital depreciates, and this may mean a delay in the tax-saving of many years. Thus while our tax system makes some provision for comparable treatment of gains and losses, the symmetry is less than complete, and to some extent the tax does have the effect of making investment a "Tails you win, heads I lose" proposition.

The significance of the reduction of the expected return and the incomplete loss offset for investment depend on the motivations of business in making investments. If a corporation is to prosper in the long run, it must maintain its position in the industry. This generates great pressure to invest to meet growing markets and to cut costs, even if a fraction of the profit goes to the government. Also, since all corporations (with certain exceptions) have to pay the tax, the after-tax rate of return which is open to investors anywhere in the economy is reduced, so that each company is able to attract capital about as well as it would without the tax. Finally, there remains a large question mark about the shifting of the tax; to the extent that the tax is shifted, the arguments do not apply, of course.

THE CORPORATION INCOME TAX
AND THE SUPPLY OF INVESTIBLE FUNDS

The tax is also important because it affects the internal supply of a company's capital. Most industrial corporations rely chiefly on internally raised capital for their expansion. They are reluctant to borrow money or to sell additional stock because the cost may be high, and the outsiders who supply the capital may limit the future actions of management. Corporations are usually anxious to reinvest the capital they generate internally—the depreciation allowances and retained profits—but will go outside the company for capital only when the investment opportunities are exceptionally attractive. The corporation income tax takes away a share of the internal funds, the kind of capital most likely to be reinvested.

This effect of the tax on the supply of funds is particularly important for new and growing enterprises. It is especially difficult for them to raise outside capital since they are not well-known and are regarded as particularly risky. If a relatively new company has developed a new product, it must expand rapidly if it is to succeed; otherwise older companies will imitate their product and take over the market. By absorbing up to half of all the profits, the tax greatly reduces the rate of expansion possible from internal capital. To illustrate, suppose a new company with a successful product earns 40 per cent on its capital and suppose that it starts with an investment of $100. It earns $40 the first year, which it reinvests; it earns $56 the second year, $78 the third year, and so on. By the end of the seventh year, the company would have total capital of $1,053. With a tax of 50 per cent, the first year's profits would be only $20, the second year's, $24, the third year's, $29, and so on. And if all of it is again reinvested, the value at the end of the seventh year would be $358. So you see that the tax prevents the kind of rapid build-up of capital which a new, expanding company requires.

As a result of this difficulty in accumulating capital internally with the present corporation income tax, as well as other tax factors,[6] many small, growing firms sell out to large established companies and disappear. This is a serious matter for the economy because we depend on the rise of new companies to keep the old giants on their toes and to keep the top corporate ranks open.

THE TAX TREATMENT OF DEPRECIATION

One of the costs subtracted from gross revenue before computing income is depreciation, the cost of the deterioration of physical capital. If depreciation accounting is skipped, as was widely practiced before 1920, income will be overstated, since, sooner or later, the equipment or the building will lose its usefulness and value. Depreciation accounting tries to solve the problem of allocating the cost of durable capital items to specific years, so that net income, after allowing for capital deterioration, can be properly identified.

The measurement of depreciation is difficult. How much of a machine should be written off in the first year and how much in other years? An engineering approach that measures physical wear and increasing maintenance costs could be tried, but this overlooks economic obsolescence, the fact that better machines become available, and that the demand for the product may disappear.

In the absence of a logical solution, simple rules of thumb have come into universal use. Most commonly, the historical cost of physical capital has been allocated in equal amounts to each year of its economic life, so that the value of an item, as recorded on the balance sheet, declines by the same amount each year. This procedure is called the *straightline method* of depreciation.

In recent decades businessmen became dissatisfied with this method as they discovered that the economic value of machines declined faster than proportionately over time. In the used-equipment market, a 1-year-old machine is worth much less than a new one; later on, value declines more slowly. Businessmen also found that for investment to be successful, they had to recoup a good part of their cost during the early years of economic life.

Depreciation accounting is especially important from the point of view of taxation. Since it is a deduction from corporate income, every dollar of extra depreciation represents a tax saving of 52 cents. If the depreciation method allowed by the tax authorities is too slow, the government is taxing

---

[6] Personal income and estate taxes also push small companies into mergers. If a successful entrepreneur were to draw income from his business, he would have to pay the high personal rates. The only way he can withdraw his wealth from the business without paying the personal tax is by selling the business and reaping a capital gain, which will then be taxed at a more favorable rate.

To pay estate taxes, a business must be liquid, but a growing company keeps its capital in equipment, inventories, and buildings, not in cash. All too frequently, the founder of the business anticipates this difficulty by merging with a larger company in exchange for stock which is marketable. (The government has attempted to give some relief to this problem by letting an estate pay the duty on a business over a 10-year period.)

more than the actual income of the business; or to put it in another way, the government takes its share of profits earlier than they are really earned. Since most firms are heavily dependent on their internal supply of funds for investment, this is a serious matter in terms of company growth. It becomes especially acute in a period of inflation, when even the best depreciation method based on historical cost does not provide sufficient funds to replace the equipment at its now inflated price.

For these reasons the government encouraged the use of two more liberal standard depreciation methods in 1954. These are the *declining balance* and the *sum-of-the-years digit* methods. But even the 1954 depreciation reforms did not prove adequate. The tax laws of our chief competitors abroad in Western Europe and Japan were more generous than our own, giving an advantage to their companies in the highly competitive interna-

FIG. 8   Three methods of depreciation: an example.

METHOD	DEPRECIATION				
	Year 1	Year 2	Year 3	Year 4	Year 5
Straightline	$\frac{1}{5}$ $20	$\frac{1}{5}$ $20	$\frac{1}{5}$ $20	$\frac{1}{5}$ $20	$\frac{1}{5}$ $20
Double declining balance	Initially twice straightline $\frac{2}{5}$ $40	$\frac{2}{5}$ of remaining balance $(\frac{2}{5} \cdot \frac{3}{5})$ $\frac{6}{25}$ $24	$(\frac{2}{5} \cdot \frac{9}{25})$ $\frac{18}{125}$ $14.44	$(\frac{2}{5} \cdot \frac{27}{125})$ $\frac{54}{625}$ $8.64	$(\frac{2}{5} \cdot \frac{81}{625})$* $\frac{162}{3,125}$ $5.18
Sum-of-the-years digits	$\frac{5}{5+4+3+2+1}$ $= \frac{5}{15}$ $33.33	$\frac{4}{5+4+3+2+1}$ $= \frac{4}{15}$ $26.67	$\frac{3}{5+4+3+2+1}$ $= \frac{3}{15}$ $20	$\frac{2}{5+4+3+2+1}$ $= \frac{2}{15}$ $13.33	$\frac{1}{5+4+3+2+1}$ $= \frac{1}{15}$ $6.67

Initial cost = $100;   Economic life = 5 years

*Because the declining balance method never completes a write-off, the government allows a switch to the straightline method at some point.

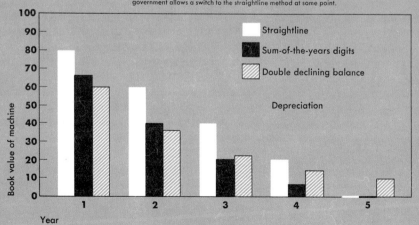

tional markets; [7] and so in 1962 the United States took additional steps. Instead of fixing the economic life of thousands of individual items of equipment, a "guideline life" was established for each industry which could be applied to all equipment—a great administrative simplification—with the guideline life set sufficiently liberally to permit most businesses to shorten average economic lives and to write off assets faster.

THE INVESTMENT CREDIT

Eager to encourage investment, the United States adopted a new device in 1962. It permits firms to deduct each year from their tax liability 7 per cent of their total current investment outlays on equipment. Thus, in effect, the government pays a subsidy on investments by giving back to firms a fraction of the investment cost through this special tax credit. This method was adopted because it is a particularly powerful incentive for stimulating growth per dollar of tax revenue lost. The tax relief directly benefits those firms willing to invest.

The investment credit was criticized on the grounds that it was a deliberate departure from tax neutrality. The tax system was being used to get businessmen to change their decisions, to undertake more investment than their ordinary judgment would dictate. Thus, this was a very explicit attempt by the government to interfere in the private economy in a manner designed to raise the rate of growth.

The Tax System and Personal Saving

While business saving is the most important source of capital for industry, personal saving also makes a contribution. Rapidly growing enterprises as well as public utilities with their enormous capital requirements must look outside their businesses, to the capital market, for both equity and debt capital. It is personal saving, the saving of households, which must provide the bulk of the long-term funds available in the capital market.

The marginal propensity to save is higher for families with larger incomes. In fact, as a whole, lower- and middle-income families do not save a great deal; furthermore, their savings tend to be channeled into home mortgages (through their banks and life insurance companies) or into government bonds. Thus, industry depends largely on the savings of a relatively small number of upper-income families. A strongly progressive income tax falls particularly heavily on this very group of people. Here, then, is another potential area in which the tax system can retard economic growth.

Professors Butters, Thompson, and Bollinger of the Harvard Business School investigated whether the personal income tax had affected personal saving. They interviewed 750 active investors, most of them in the crucial high-income brackets. They found that the tax structure had "substantially reduced the capacity of upper bracket individuals to accumulate new investible funds, but that . . . their remaining capacity is still very large." [8]

[7] France has developed the art of the tax treatment of depreciation to the highest point. Special treatment is accorded industries in which the government wants to invest heavily, such as export industries. Also, the capital was adjusted by a revaluation factor which raised depreciation allowances to offset the effects of inflation.

[8] J. K. Butters, L. E. Thompson, and L. L. Bollinger, *Effects of Taxation on Investments by Individuals*, Harvard Graduate School of Business Administration, 1953, p. 29.

More importantly, the study found that the pattern of investment was very much affected, with most investors acknowledging that they had rearranged their investment behavior because of tax considerations. On the whole, the tax system tended to polarize investors into one of two types: (1) Those who originally were income- and security-minded tended to buy tax-exempt bonds of state and local governments and life insurance policies, as the extra income to be gained from other securities was shrunk by taxes. (2) Those investors who were appreciation-minded, on the other hand, were made more willing to take risks, and placed their capital into such ventures as speculative common stocks held for capital gains, real estate benefiting from liberal depreciation allowances, and oil properties receiving the depletion allowance.

Thus, the retarding effects on saving of the high progressive rates of the personal income tax are mitigated by the special tax treatment accorded some particular kinds of investments. The adjustments of investment behavior to the tax structure have continued to make venture capital available from personal saving. This is a crucial point for the growth of the economy. The private investor, however, is not free to consider all opportunities on their merit and then to choose those which he considers to be the most promising. Instead, he is pulled and pushed by the tax structure out of and into certain kinds of investments. And apart from the general departures from a rational allocation of personal investments, it has brought about some specific side-effects which have been a mixed blessing. On the one hand, the inducement to buy tax-exempt state and local securities has provided a market for the great volume of bonds that states and localities have had to issue to finance their rising education and other costs. On the other hand, the preoccupation with capital gains rather than dividend income accentuates the speculative elements in the stock market. Similarly, the shaky boom of real estate values of recent times is heavily tax-induced.

Too Much Income Taxation?
The Search for Alternatives

While no one piece of evidence or one line of argument clearly shows our personal and corporate income taxes to have really serious retarding effects on the performance of the economy, there is sufficient uneasiness about the issue to have led some observers—and some pressure groups—to search for major alternative sources of revenue. These are some of the recent proposals:

A value-added tax. The value-added tax has been advanced as a substitute for all, or part, of the corporation income tax. France pioneered this tax, and it is possible that the European Economic Community as a whole will adopt it as its major business tax. Its base is the "value added" of each business, defined as the total value of output minus the value of purchased material inputs; this is equal to profits plus interest plus depreciation plus total labor costs. Thus, the tax has a broader base than profits. Levied only on corporations, it could raise as much money as our present corporate income tax with a rate only about one-third as high. It could also be applied to a wider range of businesses, including cooperatives and other unincorporated enterprises, thus making possible even lower rates through a broader base.

The tax has some theoretical advantages. It taxes all factors of production at the same rate, unlike the corporation income tax which is a tax on the return to capital only. Thus it does not lead to distortions in business choices about the optimal combination of the factors of production. Whereas the corporation income tax leads to a less-than-optimal use of capital by taxing that factor and not others, the value-added tax is neutral in this regard. It would encourage the substitution of capital for labor, because it would ease the tax on capital and impose a tax on labor: Labor-saving investments would be made more attractive because the cost of labor—and hence the gain from labor-saving—would be raised by that part of the tax which falls on the company's wage payments.

On the other hand, the incidence of the tax differs from the corporate tax in a regressive manner. A change from one tax to the other would, in effect, be a partial change from a tax on profits to a tax on wages. Some of the incidence of the tax would fall on the workers. Furthermore, the tax would be more likely to be passed on in higher prices and hence be shifted to consumers, Finally—and this is where the objectives of efficiency and equity clash most clearly—the value-added tax would fall relatively more heavily on unsuccessful companies and less on successful ones. Even a company which made little or no profit would have to pay the value-added tax and might even be put out of business by it, whereas the burden on successful, high-profit companies would be eased. From the point of view of having profits available for reinvestment in the expanding sectors of the economy where profit opportunities are high, and withdrawing capital from declining sectors, the change would be desirable (though this line of argument does not apply to high profits based on monopoly rather than rising demands). But what about the social and human aspects of declining industries and depressed areas? Should the tax system be changed to make their problems more acute?

A federal sales tax. Another proposal, more commonly linked with a reduction in the progressive personal income tax rates, is the introduction of a general sales tax at the federal level. Because it would be very costly to administer such a tax at retail, it has been proposed that it be imposed at the manufacturer's or wholesaler's level, where far fewer returns would be required. A tax of 2 per cent would raise enough revenue to permit elimination of most of the progression in the income tax.

This type of change would convert our present tax system of some mild progression into one that would, over all, be regressive. Apart from these equity considerations, the chief objection to the tax comes from the concern about the fiscal conditions of the states, for whom general sales taxes have been an important source of revenue. With expenditure trends rising rapidly at the state and local level, we are loath to have the federal government invade such an important state-revenue source.

The expenditure tax, discussed earlier in connection with the proper measure of ability to pay, has also received some attention in the U.S. By taxing only consumption, not saving, it could raise the fraction of personal income which is saved. It has not enjoyed wide support in the U.S. because a shortage of personal saving has not been considered a major obstacle to growth in recent years. Furthermore, if given a progressive rate structure, it would reduce the economy's efficiency at least as much as an income tax, perhaps more, since the rates would have to be higher to yield the same revenues.

The Tax System and the Growth of Demand

In the preceding section we have discussed the relation of the tax system to the growth of the economy's capacity to produce. We assumed that more effort means more output, more saving leads to more investment and more productive capacity. Thus, we looked at growth only from the point of view of the potential supply of output, not the demand for output. But to achieve growth, both supply and demand must grow at a proper rate. When demand grows too rapidly, inflation results. When demand is sluggish, unemployment and idle capacity develop. The tax system helps determine whether supply and demand grow in balance because it affects the rate of growth of both supply and demand.

As income grows, tax collections grow as well, reducing the growth of purchasing power and effective demand. Not all taxes respond in the same proportions. For example, a progressive income tax will rise faster than income because taxpayers enter higher brackets, so that not only the tax base but also the average effective tax rate increases. Gasoline, liquor, and tobacco excises rise much less than income because the amount of consumption of these items responds only mildly to income growth.

It would be sheer chance if the revenue response of the tax system to growth were precisely such as to keep the growth of supply and demand in balance. Corrective policies to maintain this balance—that is, to maintain full employment without excess demand, are the subject of Chapter 6. Here let us only keep in mind that measures designed to improve the structure of the tax system for the sake of growth of supply can be nullified if the aggregate response of tax collections to economic growth is too severe, keeping demand too low.

Concluding Comments

The American tax system does not fit any simple ideal scheme. It grew up helter-skelter over many decades, with some of the most important changes made quickly to meet sudden needs for extra revenue. It has its loopholes and its structural faults. It is easy to recommend improvements; you might draw up your own list of proposed changes. But basically the United States has a very strong tax system, one which has allowed our economy to flourish. Considering that the total taxes collected are over 25 per cent of gross national product, it is surprising that the tax system does so little visible damage to the performance of the economy. Needless to say, we should continue to strive to improve it, to keep the tax system up-to-date and responsive to changing economic conditions and objectives. But I think that when all is said and done, one has to conclude that it is an extraordinarily effective system, and one of the main sources of our nation's strength. It has succeeded in giving the government the great command over resources which it has needed to meet its enormous responsibilities to defend and develop the free world, and to carry out its assigned functions at home.

Summary

The tax system affects the efficiency of resource allocation within the economy. A selective system of excise taxes, for example, upsets the marginal conditions necessary for an efficient resource allocation by confronting producers with a different set of relative prices from that faced by consumers. The personal income tax affects the supply of labor, particularly upper-bracket income-earners paying high marginal rates. Empirical studies so far suggest that these effects are moderate. Executive mobility has, however, been impaired, and much effort is wasted on tax avoidance.

The tax system also affects the growth of the economy. The corporation income tax affects the incentive to invest and the supply of investible funds. Some important measures have been taken in recent years to ameliorate these effects, including liberalization of depreciation allowances and an investment credit.

Finally, the tax system affects the amount of personal saving and investment. Its influence on the patterns of personal investment behavior is probably more important than its effects on total personal saving and investment.

Although no one single retarding effect has been discovered which would justify a drastic rearrangement of our tax system, many people feel that the federal government relies too heavily on income taxation. Several major alternative sources of revenue have been proposed. These include the value-added tax, a federal sales tax, and an expenditure tax.

7

BUDGET POLICY FOR ECONOMIC STABILITY

So far, this book has been chiefly concerned with the long-term objectives of economic policy, equity, efficiency, and growth. But much of public finance is concerned with short-run matters—the influence of the federal budget on total purchasing power, the use of the budget to fight recession and inflation. Changes in taxes and expenditures which aim at the short-run goals of full employment and price-level stability are usually called *fiscal policy*. This chapter examines the theory of fiscal policy, which derives from the general framework of national income analysis.[1] Qualifications to the theory and the actual fiscal policy of recent years are also examined.

The Theory of Fiscal Policy

To see the role of government budgets in relation to the determination of the short-run output of the economy, let us first recall the determination of national income in the hypothetical situation in which there is no government budget. Figure 9 summarizes the national income determination process. Line *CC* is the consumption function, which shows the consumption expenditures which will be made out of different levels of income. There will also be some specific level of investment, and if we add this amount to the consumption function (*C* + *I*), we get the total level of spending, or "effective demand," generated out of each level of income. The equilibrium level of GNP, where total spending by households and businesses equals total income and production, is the point *a* in Fig. 9. The full employment level of GNP is *OD,* so that the equilibrium level falls below full employment in this example.

Suppose we now bring government expenditures into the analysis. They will be an addition to effective demand. However, the taxes which are also part of the budget reduce private spending. Personal taxes reduce disposable income directly, and taxes shifted to the consumer via higher prices reduce the real value of income. Consequently, the consumption function—here defined as relating consumption to GNP—is shifted downward. Furthermore, taxes also reduce investment. Thus the total spending line is shifted downward by the reduction in consumption and investment, upward by the government spending.

The budget can raise or lower the equilibrium level of GNP compared

[1] See Charles L. Schultze, *National Income Analysis,* this Series, especially Chapters 2 and 3.

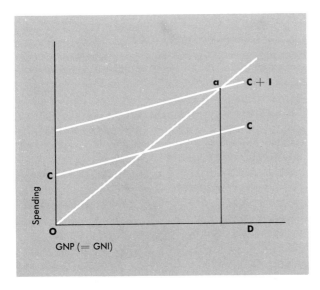

FIG. 9 National income determination process.

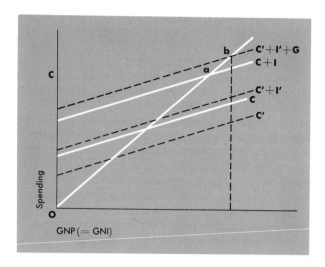

FIG. 10 Equilibrium level of GNP compared to a hypothetical no-government situation.

to the hypothetical no-government situation. Figure 10 shows the new equilibrium. C' is the consumption function after taxes have cut disposable income, $C' + I'$ adds the reduced investment, while $C' + I' + G$ adds the government expenditure to derive the total spending line. The equilibrium GNP is equal to b, which happens to turn out to be greater than the level a of the no-government case, showing the budget to be a positive influence on effective demand. But this result depends on the magnitude of expenditures and taxes, and on their characteristics.

The fiscal policy implications of national income analysis can be expressed as a series of propositions:

An increase in government expenditures raises GNP. The size of this increase is determined by the multiplier. The additional dollar of government expenditures purchases a dollar of goods and services and becomes the income of households (wages, interest, and rent), of businessmen (profits), and of government (additional tax revenue). Some of these incomes will be re-spent, the exact amount depending on the marginal spending propensities of the spenders. Assuming, just for the moment, that neither business nor government spend any of their extra income, and assuming that households spend 90 cents out of every additional dollar of income, we get the following sequence. Let business and government receive 40 cents out of the dollar of extra expenditure. Consumers will spend nine-tenths of the remaining 60 cents, or 54 cents. Assume that these 54 cents of consumption spending will again be divided in the same pattern, yielding households an additional 32 cents of income; they will spend 29 cents for consumption in the next round, and so on. The total effect will be $1 + 54¢ + 29¢ + 16¢ + . . . , a total of $2.18. Thus for every additional dollar of government expenditures, total GNP is increased by $2.18. And remember that no allowance was made for additional investment out of the increased profits, or for more government spending out of the extra tax revenues. Figure 11 shows this multiplier process, with the numerals indicating the succeeding rounds as the new equilibrium level of GNP is approached.

An increase in taxes reduces GNP. The size of the decrease depends on the multiplier. Suppose that taxes are increased by a dollar, falling proportionately on household and business income. Households will pay 60 cents, businesses 40 cents. Consumer spending will fall 54 cents in the first round, 29 cents in the second, and so on, as in the preceding example. The resultant sequence, 54¢ + 29¢ + 16¢ + . . . , adds up to a total multiplier on a tax change of $1.18.

Notice that this tax multiplier is just 1 less than the expenditure multiplier (and of opposite sign, of course). This result has a simple explanation. The repercussion effects after the first round are the same; but the government purchase of goods and services was a direct component of effective demand and of GNP, whereas the initial round of the tax payment was simply a transfer of purchasing power, which does not count as GNP. The precise numerical difference between the expenditure and tax multipliers of 1 depends on the assumption that the same marginal propensity to consume applies to the taxpayers as to the income recipients of the government expenditures; and as we shall see below, that is an assumption that is not likely to hold precisely. Nevertheless, it is an important truth that $1 of taxation does not neutralize $1 of expenditures. Unlike the government expenditure, part of the taxes would have been saved rather than spent, and a multiplier has to be applied to this difference. Thus we add a third principle: *A balanced increase in the level of a budget, with both expenditures and taxes rising by the same amount, changes the level of GNP, normally raising it.*

The Budget Principles of Fiscal Theory

Fiscal theory contains a set of prescriptions for budget policy. When Gross National Product is below the full employment level, budget policy should become more *expansionary*. This can be done by reducing tax rates or by increasing expenditures; either measure will increase total effective demand. When total demand for output is too high—that is, when the total level of spending exceeds the full employment rate of GNP, causing inflation—the budget must be made more *restrictive* by increasing tax rates or reducing expenditure programs.

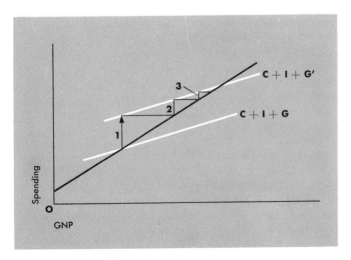

FIG. 11 The multiplier process.

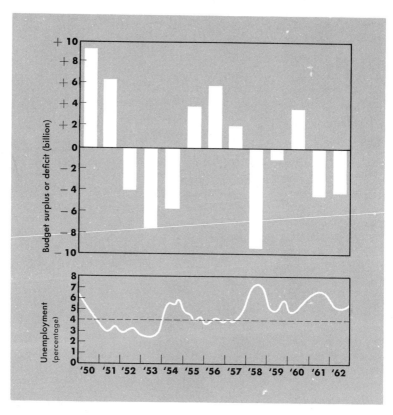

FIG. 12 Federal budget surpluses and deficits.

In any specific situation, these principles still leave open the choice between tax and expenditure changes. For example, in the case of a necessary expansion of demand, should taxes be cut or expenditures increased? Lower taxes will mean more private spending, increased expenditures more public spending. Which route to full employment is to be preferred in a particular situation depends on the evaluation of the relative merits of public and private spending, an issue we took up in Chapter 1. Practical questions of immediate feasibility also have to be considered.

Deficits and Surpluses: Automatic and Discretionary Changes

The actual record of the federal budget (as presented in the National Income and Product Accounts) is shown in Fig. 12, along with the unemployment rate. You can see that huge deficits were incurred in recession, a mixture of smaller surpluses and deficits at the other times. Since deficits represent additions to total spending (the government adds more through spending than it subtracts through taxation), the movements in the budget have, broadly speaking, added to economic stability. But in interpreting the raw deficit and surplus figures, this distinction has to be kept in mind:

Some of the changes in the budget are automatic; others are discretion-

ary. As GNP falls, incomes and sales decline, automatically cutting government revenues. Some categories of expenditures, particularly unemployment and relief benefits, automatically increase in response to a decline in GNP. Thus, a decline in GNP pushes the budget toward deficit, and conversely for a rise in GNP. As a rule of thumb, for every billion dollars of extra GNP, the federal budget gains about $300 million of extra surplus or reduced deficit. Figure 13, line *AA'*, shows this relationship.

The taxes and expenditures that exhibit this response markedly have been called *automatic stabilizers*. Although they place the government in deficit, they serve as a cushion for private purchasing power. Back in the 1920's, before unemployment insurance, a substantial corporate profits tax, and a broadly levied income tax, there was much less automatic stabilization in the federal budget. This change is perhaps the most significant cause of the increased stability of the economy today, and the strongest insurance against another major depression.

The budget can also be changed by *discretionary policies* of government, such as altering tax rates or expenditure programs. A discretionary change alters the relationship between budget surpluses and deficits and the levels of GNP. In Fig. 13 a discretionary change leads to a new line, *BB'*. If the change is restrictive (e.g., an increase in tax rates or a reduction in an expenditure program), the new line will lie above the old line; for any given level of economic activity, the surplus will be greater (or the deficit smaller).

The Full Employment Budget

Because the actual budget surplus or deficit in a period is the result both of movements in the economy and of discretionary policies, one cannot distinguish actual budget policy from the historical record of surpluses and deficits. To disentangle these two causes, the concept of the full employment sur-

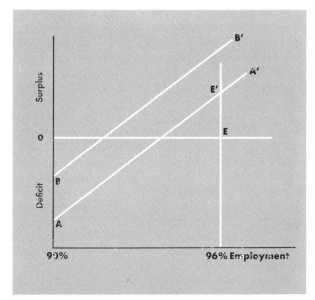

FIG. 13 Effect of discretionary change on the budget.

plus (or deficit) has been invented. It refers to the surplus or deficit in the budget which would occur if the economy were at full employment. The difference between the full employment surplus and the actual surplus or deficit is then attributable to the automatic budget response to the deviations of the economy from the full employment level. In Fig. 13 the vertical line *EE'* measures this full employment surplus. By comparing full employment surpluses of different budget structures, one can see just how restrictive or expansionary these budgets are. Thus the more restrictive budget policy *BB'* produces a full employment surplus which is greater than *EE'*.[2] (Full employment is usually defined as the condition where unemployment is no greater than the normal and frictional unemployment of 3 to 4 per cent; a normal utilization rate of industrial capacity is also considered in sophisticated estimates of "full employment" GNP.)

Figure 14 shows the full employment surpluses of the last 10 years. You can see that if there had been continuous full employment, the federal budget would have been in surplus from 1954 on. The full employment surplus moved counter-cyclically, but very much less so than the actual budget surpluses and deficits. Outside of the recessions, the surpluses were large, making the private economy operate under a significant, retarding influence.

[2] The comparisons can be ambiguous if the slopes of the lines differ, possibly with the lines crossing. But it turns out that for the usual kinds of discretionary budget changes, such as changing tax rates or increasing expenditures, the slope of the line is not very much affected, but rather the curve is shifted in a close to parallel manner.

FIG. 14   Full employment surpluses, 1954-1962.

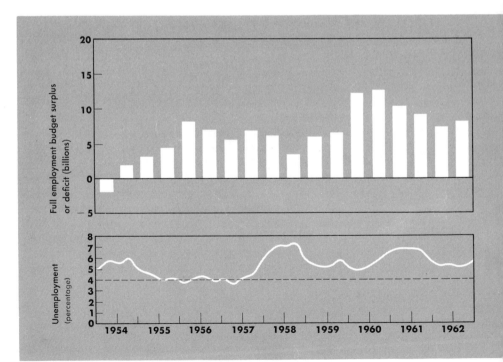

Some Complications

The prescriptions of fiscal theory are straightforward enough—cut taxes, raise expenditures to expand the economy; raise taxes, cut expenditures to contract it. The multiplier reveals how large the changes must be to reach full employment at stable prices. Then why is there so much controversy about fiscal policies? And why don't we follow the rules and avoid unemployment and inflation? Before we leave this subject we had best examine some of the qualifications to the theory, some practical difficulties of implementing it, and some of the other ideas and budget principles that are being advanced in the continuing national debate over our national budget.

Not all expenditures have the same multiplier effects. Transfer payments do not constitute a direct demand for goods and services. Just as a part of taxes reduce saving rather than spending, so part of the transfer expenditures become the equivalent of saving. The recipients may not be able to put the money in the bank, but they may well have outstanding debts on their homes, their cars, and their appliances, and may have to use part of the benefits to repay their obligations. With that initial round of assured direct purchase of goods and services absent, a lower multiplier is likely.[3]

Nor will the households through whom the various rounds of the multiplier pass all have the same marginal propensity to consume. We know that upper-income families save more, so that the multiplier may be larger or smaller, depending on who receives the income. During the Great Depression, there was some belief that the economy could be stimulated significantly simply by redistributing income—taxing the upper-income, high-saving groups, paying benefits to low-income, low-saving groups. The resultant effect on spending was called the *redistribution multiplier*. Empirical studies, on the whole, have cast doubt on the possibilities of this procedure. Marginal propensities to consume are high rather far up the income scale, through all the brackets that have millions of people in them, and the amount of income that could be redistributed from the high-saving groups is small.

Perhaps more important are differences in the fraction of expenditures that reach households as disposable income. In our earlier example, we assumed that only 60 cents of each expenditure dollar would reach households, the rest being absorbed by taxes and retained corporate earnings. That figure will vary, depending on the form of expenditure, with labor-intensive projects—including make-work projects like leaf-raking—having a somewhat stronger effect on household disposable income than defense spending or heavy public works.

Some government expenditures are for imports. Their multiplier effects occur not in the United States, but outside. This may seem like a small point, since imports represent no more than 4 per cent of our GNP; but the federal budget includes a more than proportionate share of purchases abroad, for foreign military and economic aid and to maintain our own overseas forces.

Some government expenditures will displace private expenditures, rather than add to them. For example, a government-built hydroelectric power dam

---

[3] If the transfer recipients have the same marginal propensity to consume as taxpayers, a balanced increase of taxes and transfer payments would have no effect on total demand whatsoever.

inevitably displaces some private investment that would have been made to meet the power needs of the area. When the government purchases home mortgages in large quantities to stimulate house-building, as it has frequently done in periods of recession, many of these mortgages would have been financed privately, and the homes that were financed would have been built anyway.

Government spending may also jolt business confidence. In the 1930's widespread fear was expressed that the sheer growth of government and the possibility of coming nationalization would discourage business from investing. Although still talked about, this factor is now probably of lesser importance, because we have all grown accustomed to big government. Nowadays, when more government spending is indicated, business investment plans are more likely to respond favorably; that most cold-blooded indicator of business psychology, the stock market, is pretty sure to bounce up. Furthermore, the knowledge that the government does have responsibility for moderating the business cycle shores up business confidence.

Not all tax changes have the same multiplier effects. Just as in the case of expenditures, differences in the marginal propensities to consume among the tax cut recipients may affect the magnitude of the multiplier. As long as the tax cut is not concentrated in the very top brackets, this is not likely to be important. But the specific form of the tax cut may make a difference.

There is a question whether a temporary tax cut is as effective as permanent reduction. Some economists believe that consumption out of temporary or "windfall" income is less than out of income expected to be received regularly.[4] If this is correct—and the empirical evidence found so far does not settle the issue unequivocally—then a lower multiplier has to be applied to a temporary tax cut.

Tax changes other than changes in personal income taxes do not fit the fiscal theory of the multiplier so neatly, and other analyses must be added. For example, an increase in sales tax rates involves other issues. First, to whom is the burden of the tax shifted? If the tax is borne by consumers, it reduces their real purchasing power just like an income tax. Some of the burden of the excise tax may be shifted to the workers producing the taxed product through lower wage payments, and this part of the tax burden is also like an income tax. Some of the tax may fall on the profits of the industry. This will lead to a reduction in investment and of consumption by the owners of the business, but the amount need not be the same as that suggested by the multiplier based on the marginal propensity to consume of the average household. Furthermore, since it is a tax on consumption only and thus exempts saving, this form of tax may lead consumers to substitute saving for consumption, thus producing an additional cut in spending.

Suppose the tax changed is the corporation income tax. First, the shifting and incidence problem has to be resolved. Who really pays—the business, the consumer, or the worker? This is still an unsettled question. In so far as the incidence falls on business profits, the initial effect on spending will not depend on the multiplier which measures consumption effects, but on the influence of corporate profits on investment (see Chapter 6). Does an extra dollar of corporation income tax reduce investment by

[4] This position is advanced in M. Friedman, *The Theory of the Consumption Function,* National Bureau of Economic Research, 1957. See Schultze, *National Income Analysis,* this Series, for a discussion of this issue.

10 cents or by a dollar? So far it has proved virtually impossible to find a precise answer to this question. We do know that the effect will be greater when business is short of investible funds in relation to investment opportunities than when corporations have a great deal of liquid assets. But there are no simple rules governing how liquidity changes over the business cycle; sometimes businesses are most short of investible funds during a boom when investment opportunities are very favorable and the interest cost of borrowing is high; at other times, they are more pinched for funds during a recession, when profits are low. Thus the effect of this kind of tax change on total spending depends on the circumstances during a particular period and cannot be ascertained precisely.

The financing of deficits can have a restrictive effect. Suppose that government is fighting a recession by raising expenditures and cutting taxes, thereby creating a sizable deficit. This deficit has to be financed somehow, since government, like anyone else, has to pay its bills. It can get money by printing it; but a responsible government refuses to engage in that simple maneuver even though it has the legal power to do so. Or it can sell securities, by going to the capital market like any other borrower. When it does so, it competes with private investment by making it more difficult for private borrowers to obtain investible funds. In a period of tight credit, private borrowing may be substantially decreased by government borrowing. The negative multipliers on the reduction of private investment may offset a significant part of the positive multipliers arising from the government's tax and spending policy.

Usually, this offset will be small. The Federal Reserve System will have the same policy goals as the rest of the government, and when the budget is put into deficit to stimulate the economy, the Reserve System will be pursuing an easy money policy. It will keep bank reserves ample through open-market operations or reduced reserve requirements, thus making it possible for both private and public borrowers to obtain funds readily and at moderate interest cost. Nevertheless, if the Federal Reserve works at cross purposes with the Treasury and the Budget Bureau, it can offset part of the stimulating effect of reduced taxes or higher expenditures.

Practical difficulties: time lags. The delays in diagnosing recessions and inflations, and of then devising and executing fiscal policy measures to combat them are perhaps the biggest obstacle to the effective use of discretionary fiscal policies. First, there is the *recognition lag*, the several months which pass before analysts agree that a recession or an inflation in fact exists. Ideally, one would wish to anticipate stabilization problems before they have arisen—that is, to forecast recession or inflation and then take positive steps. But so far we have never based stabilization policy on forecasts, only on diagnosis of events that have already transpired. The *decision lag* follows, the months during which the president and his advisers make up their minds just what to do, the period of consideration by the Congress, plus the additional months in which the expenditure programs are actually planned in detail and the money then gradually spent, or in which the tax changes actually become effective. Finally, there is the *expenditure lag*, the period before the full economic impact of the successive multiplier rounds takes place.

Lags have proved so troublesome for some kinds of programs that we have pretty much given them up as potential weapons in our counter-cyclical arsenal. Large-scale public works, such as dams, take months to design; the condemnation proceedings to acquire the necessary land may take years, and the period of construction will add more years. With recessions typically running their course in a relatively few months, it is impossible to achieve significant and timely spending effects through this method. Tax changes face no such technical obstacles, but the process of tax legislation is so slow in peacetime that this instrument has seen very little use as a stabilization device.

Monetary policy encounters shorter decision and execution lags. Little time need be taken to devise the specific measures, since they are traditional and clearly defined. And the Federal Reserve can engage in open-market operations without consulting Congress, or even other government agencies. Thus, monetary policy encounters only two lags of any substance—the recognition lag, which is pretty much the same as for fiscal policy; and the expenditure lag, which may be even greater than for fiscal policy, because the easing of credit need not have immediate effects on actual spending.

Practical difficulties: forecasting errors. Diagnosis of stabilization problems may not only be tardy but also may be wrong. The ups and downs of the post-war business cycle have been so slight and sudden that it has been difficult to predict them accurately. Swings in business inventory policy have been the single most important manifestation of post-war cycles, although variations in fixed business investment and government purchases have usually been the more fundamental causes. Today, short-run forecasters closely follow dozens of statistical indicators which show the direction of movement of the economy, and construct elaborate economic models to discover the coming business-cycle patterns. Nevertheless, forecasting remains an uncertain art. Discretionary fiscal policies, if they are to contribute to economic stability through quick action, should be based on correct forecasts. If analysts could foresee the coming recession or inflation, preventive policies could be pursued.

In fact, few have succeeded in predicting turning points in the business cycle. The best that we have been able to do so far is to diagnose them promptly after they have happened. This forecasting difficulty has led some observers to conclude that fiscal policy should rely primarily on automatic stabilizers, which swing into action without explicit diagnosis through the working of the economy itself, rather than on discretionary policies which may be pursued on the basis of incorrect forecasts. However, discretionary policies undertaken after the recession (or inflation) has been diagnosed can still contribute to economic stability if undertaken promptly.

Conflicts between full employment and price-level stability. What should fiscal policy be when unemployment rises above the normal levels, yet prices are rising at the same time? This situation should not occur in a smoothly functioning competitive economy, since price levels should be stable or falling when the total demand for goods and services does not exceed the total supply. (Presumably unemployment can be above normal only when total demand for output falls short of potential supply.) In terms of Fig. 9, the full employment point, *D*, should neatly separate the GNP levels which are inflationary from the rest.

In the post-war period, however, we have repeatedly had the unfortunate experience of having both unemployment and inflation occur; only in brief transitional periods have prices been stable at normal unemployment levels. This is not the place to explore the causes of this situation. Rapid changes in the composition of final demand which strained the adjustment capabilities of industry were certainly one factor. Some blame the monopoly power of business, others of unions. Some contend that technological change has made many workers' skills obsolete, leaving them unemployed even in a state of general excess demand.[5]

But whatever the cause, the problem that is thereby posed for fiscal policy is one that is impossible to solve. Fiscal policy cannot, at the same time, both promote full employment by adding to total spending and fight inflation by subtracting from it. What then to do? Essentially, this dilemma forces the government to choose between the two objectives: Does the government consider full employment or stability of prices more important? This is a philosophical rather than a technical question, and it depends on the president and the Congress and the temper of the times how the choice is resolved. If the situation is further complicated by difficulties in our international balance of payments, price-level stability may take precedence.

This difficulty of conflicting objectives is not a criticism of the traditional fiscal and monetary tools of stabilization policy. The fault lies elsewhere, in the structure of the economy. Other policies, such as reduction of monopoly power and improvement in the mobility of labor and of other productive factors, are then needed which will reconcile the objectives, leaving to the policies acting on total spending a task which they can accomplish —namely, the promotion of the "correct" level of demand which produces full employment without inflation.

Other Budget Principles: The Annually Balanced Budget

Modern fiscal theory requires that at some times the budget be in surplus, at others in deficit. Only by accident would precise balance be the exactly correct budget policy. Yet the idea of balancing expenditures with revenues for every year continues to have immense appeal, and crops up without end in speeches and on editorial pages. Even political leaders who understand and accept modern fiscal theory find themselves very much on the defensive when the budget is in deficit.

Why do the older ideas die so slowly? Do they possibly contain some germ of validity? One thing is certain. If the federal government pursued a rigid budget-balancing policy, insisting on precise balance each year regardless of the movements in the private economy, it would lead to disaster. It would mean that tax rates would be increased and expenditures slashed in recession, and taxes cut and spending increased in inflation. In the early days of the Great Depression, both Presidents Hoover and Roosevelt deliberately sought to restore a budget balance, even as unemployment grew very large. They raised taxes in 1932, 1934 and 1935, and enforced strict economy in the ordinary budget. A humane response to the desperate needs of the unemployed, first by Hoover and then more extensively by Roosevelt, led them to establish various relief and public-works programs, helping to swell the depression-induced deficits. But the total discretionary fiscal policy of the 1930's, as measured by the full employment deficits and surpluses, continued to reflect the fear of unbalanced budgets and kept the government from an

---

[5] See Schultze, *National Income Analysis,* this Series, Chapter 5.

all-out anti-depression fiscal policy. This was a contributing factor to the depth and persistence of the depression.

Then why do the ideas persist? First, because we draw simple analogies between our personal finances and the government's finances. We know that when our expenditures exceed our income, we pile up debts; a day of reckoning comes when we have to cut down our standard of living to pay the creditors. In the next chapter we shall take up the true nature of the burden of a public debt; there is, indeed, a burden, but it is not of the same sort as for individual debt. Here let it suffice to point out that an increase in the federal debt involves an important consideration unique to it. The federal government is so large that one cannot overlook its impact on the economy's total income and output. To illustrate, suppose a debt-ridden individual decides to achieve a sounder financial position. He can reduce his expenditures below his income, and gradually pay off his obligations. But now suppose the federal government attempts to pursue the same policy to eliminate the national debt, say, over a period of 20 years. The surpluses that it would attempt to run would so reduce total spending and output that the economy would remain far below its capacity, produce less tax revenues, and thereby defeat the aim of retiring the debt.

It is also widely believed that the deficits cause inflation, and that to abandon the balanced budget is to let the government pursue never-ceasing inflationary policies. Now, it is true that deficits add to total demand, and in some circumstances, this will be inflationary. But increased demand should not lead to price increases so long as there is unemployed labor and idle capital; thus deficits should not be inflationary in periods of underemployment. If the economy has an inflationary bias caused by concentrations of market power in the hands of companies and unions, then deficits which restore full employment will also produce inflation. But here the trouble lies not in the deficit but in the presence of monopoly elements in the structure of the economy's markets. Government is then faced with the unpleasant choices of the unemployment-inflation dilemma. The historical record of actual government decisions shows that in fact we have not pursued full employment policies blindly, but have carefully weighed the inflationary hazards against the unemployment costs, and have chosen to live with considerable unemployment for the sake of price-level stability. Equally important from the point of view of preventing inflation when there is excess demand, the proper budget policy is not balance, but a surplus, to siphon off private purchasing power and bring total demand in line with total supply.

Another reason for the continued support of the annually balanced budget is the belief that it is the only principle which limits the growth of government expenditures. Adam Smith favored budget-balancing on these grounds. Royal borrowing helped finance wasteful court life, depriving the business classes of much-needed credit to finance the trade and investment which was the basis of economic growth. Today, it is not kings but politicians who are supposed to be "reckless spenders." Budget-balancing every year is supposed to force politicians to face up to the tax cost of expenditures, and since increases in tax rates are unpopular, it does tend to confine the expenditure rise to normal revenue growth. When expenditures rise faster than revenues, a balanced-budget rule requires legislatures to vote higher tax rates, an unpopular step they take reluctantly.

Modern fiscal principles do not provide the public with a simple, readily understood rule for evaluating total government spending, a rule which would serve as a discipline on spending decisions. It is this lack of a modern alternative yardstick which gives the older ideas their continued appeal. Once the curse is taken off deficits, as is done by modern fiscal principles, how can the public tell whether spending is reckless or not?

While budget-balancing may reduce total spending, it does not assure efficiency or an end to waste. If there is waste in government, in such fields as agriculture, stockpiling, foreign aid, or even defense, a balanced budget will not eliminate it. Wasteful expenditures, on the whole, have not resulted from general fiscal looseness, but from powerful pressure groups (both the private beneficiaries and the public bureaucracies that administer the programs) and from the lack of pressure for efficiency in the absence of competition and the profit motive.

The annually balanced budget puts a damper on government spending, but it is a heavy price to pay. It is impossible to pursue a rational policy for stability and growth under it. Nor is the discipline on spending very effective. Hardly anyone is in favor of government spending *per se*. It is always a specific program which is desired, and the proponents usually argue that it could be financed by economies in other programs. Thus, what little may be gained by controlling spending is hardly worth the cost of pursuing a fiscal policy which strongly reinforces instabilities in the private economy.

Budget-Balancing at Full Employment: The CED Plan

Recognizing that sound budget policy requires both counter-cyclical variation in surpluses and deficits as well as some principles to assure fiscal discipline, the Committee for Economic Development, an organization of outstanding business leaders, proposed in 1947 that a new budget principle be adopted. They recommended that the level of expenditures be determined on the basis of long-term merits, not short-run grounds, and that tax rates be set so that a small surplus would be produced if full employment prevailed. It was expected that this budget principle would produce a balanced budget over the full course of business cycles, with the surpluses of the booms offsetting the recession deficits.

This policy recommendation was noteworthy on several grounds. First, it indicated that a modern, counter-cyclical fiscal policy was acceptable to an important segment of the business community. Second, the policy rejects discretionary policies, and relies completely on the automatic flexibility of the budget. The CED felt that the time lags in discretionary fiscal measures were too great and forecasting errors too serious. They also felt that a discretionary fiscal policy made the environment for business decisions more uncertain, as businessmen, besides running their ordinary risks, would have to guess about government policy. Finally, the principle preserves the requirement on politicians to balance new expenditure programs with new revenues, since the rule of a small surplus at full employment requires the matching of expenditures with revenues. In this way it was hoped that a modern counterpart of the principle of the annually balanced budget could be established.

The CED plan can be criticized. Automatic stabilization may not be enough. Depending on conditions in the private economy, the CED policy might leave the economy with substantial unemployment or inflation. When the private economy is particularly buoyant, with investment demand high, and, say, automobile sales booming, correct stabilization policy may require a large surplus in the full employment budget. When private demand is weak, stabilization may require a deficit in the full employment budget. There is no assurance that a budget which would slightly overbalance at hypothetical full employment will actually produce full employment. As for fiscal discipline, it is questionable whether wasteful expenditures are kept in check by the annually balanced budget; a hypothetical budget balance never confirmed by dollar-and-cents accounting figures would have an even slighter effect. Nevertheless, CED policy would have worked tolerably well in the last 15 years, probably better than actual policy a good part of the time. And that is not a small recommendation.[6]

Actual Fiscal Policy against Recession

Fiscal policy can be evaluated only on its actual performance. To illustrate, Fig. 15 summarizes the policy that was used to combat the 1958 recession. This figure shows the total decline of GNP from its full employment path, a maximum decline of $30 billion after three quarters, followed by a rapid recovery in the succeeding year. The federal budget swung from a surplus of $3 billion to an $11 billion deficit. This swing of $14 billion made the decline in private incomes and private purchasing power much smaller than the decline in GNP, offsetting almost half the decline in GNP.

The major part of the budget swing was due to the automatic stabilizers, which accounted for $12 of the $14 billion. Table 12 summarizes the automatic declines in tax collections and increases in unemployment benefits attributable to the recession.

TABLE 12

Automatic Stabilizers in the 1958 Recession

	Changes from Full Employment Level
Decreased revenues	
Corporation income tax	—4.9
Excise taxes	—0.8
Social insurance taxes	—0.7
Individual income taxes	—3.3
Increased expenditures	
Unemployment compensation	+2.2
Total automatic change in budget	—11.9

The full employment surplus, reflecting both discretionary policies and budget movements unrelated to recession, increased somewhat during the first quarter of the recession, accelerating the decline, but then fell steadily for a year to significantly aid the recovery. Its maximum swing was $5 billion.

[6] In particular, it would have avoided some of the large full employment surpluses that retarded the private economy in the later 1950's.

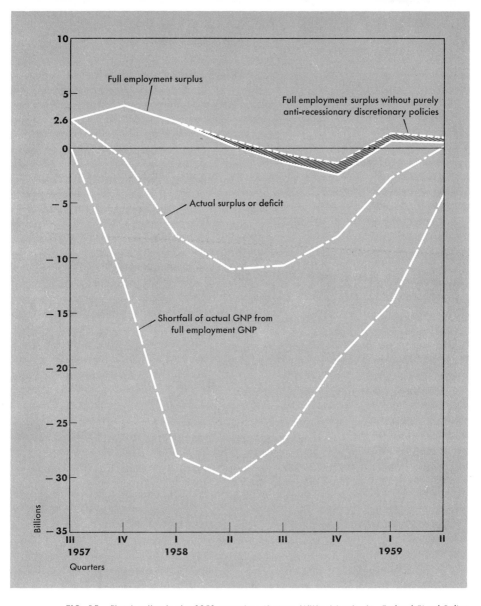

FIG. 15 Fiscal policy in the 1958 recession. (Source: Wilfred Lewis, Jr., *Federal Fiscal Policy in the Postwar Recessions*, Washington, D.C.: The Brookings Institution, 1962.)

But much of this was not deliberate anti-recession policy. The agricultural program suddenly became more costly, and other expenditures (particularly for defense and social security) rose by more than normal revenue growth. The dotted line in Fig. 15 shows what would have happened to the full employment surplus in the absence of anti-recession measures, and the shaded area just below the dotted line isolates the effect of the purely anti-recession discretionary policy. (But perhaps some of the "ordinary" increases in agriculture and defense would not have been permitted without the easy budget attitudes engendered by the recession!) Among the specific measures taken, a temporary program of extending the period of eligibility for unemployment insurance was the most important, together with special programs of mortgage purchases to boost residential construction. Various public-works programs for highways, dams, and the like, were accelerated, but the total effect of these measures was slight.

Although extensively debated, tax rates were not reduced during this recession. There was no agreement on the type of tax cut that should be made, and when the first signs of a brightening in the business-cycle picture could be seen in April, 1958, politicians sighed with relief at not having to fight over a change in the tax system, and quickly shelved plans for reduction. The failure to make tax cuts during a recession is one of the most striking characteristics of post-war fiscal policy. In none of the four recessions did the president ask for, nor the Congress enact, counter-cyclical tax changes.[7]

Fiscal policy during the 1958 recession was typical of post-war experience. The automatic stabilizers offset a substantial part of the decline in GNP. But discretionary policy proved very limited, even though the government devoted considerable ingenuity and energy toward accelerating spending programs. Most government programs serve long-run functions that have to be met regardless of the business cycle, and the actual expenditures cannot be varied significantly within the space of a few months. On the tax side, the political process proved to be a complete block to quick anti-recession action.

Actual Fiscal Policy during Inflation

The United States has experienced 3 inflations since World War II: the post-World War II inflation, the inflation during the Korean War, and the creeping inflation of the mid-fifties. Our review of fiscal policy in practice would not be complete without a quick look at its role in these episodes.

The inflation of 1945-1948 accompanied the astonishingly smooth and successful reconversion of the economy from military to civilian production. As the federal government cut the share of GNP which it absorbed from 42 per cent in 1944 to less than 7 per cent in 1947, it reduced wartime taxes substantially, but much less than expenditures. A deficit of $55 billion in 1944 was converted to a surplus of $12 billion in 1947. This enormous swing could not eliminate inflation because private demand was extremely strong. Families reunited after the war had pressing needs for housing, cars, and appliances, and they possessed the wartime savings to convert these backlogs into effective demand. Considerable inflation was suppressed in wartime through price, wage and rent controls; and when these controls were removed, wages and prices moved to new equilibrium levels. No fiscal policy could have averted this inflation, but fiscal policy made a substantial contribution in limiting the inflation and bringing it to an end.

The Korean War inflation was largely psychological. Consumers, businesses, and governments all over the world promptly hoarded commodities, driving world material prices up sharply and causing wholesale and retail prices to rise by over 10 per cent in a year. Price and wage controls were imposed, but only after much of the price increase had already occurred.

[7] However, in two cases, the recessions of 1949 and 1954, taxes were reduced counter-cyclically through good luck. In 1949 the Congress cut taxes over presidential opposition before recession was recognized. In 1954 some of the Korean War taxes were repealed effective as of a future date, a date which turned out to be near the trough of the recession.

Fiscal policy was the main instrument of anti-inflationary policy during the crucial early stages of the war. In September, 1950, both personal and corporate income tax rates were increased and an excess profits tax was imposed. A year later, as military expenditures increased, income taxes were raised once more and excise taxes on luxuries boosted. Thus, discretionary action was prompt and vigorous. It could not stop the inflation in its tracks because of the intensity of the psychological pressure, but it reduced the amount of inflation and permitted the diversion of resources to war purposes.

The inflation of the mid-fifties was in some respects the most frustrating for policy. Excess demand did not permeate the entire economy but was confined to a few sectors—the durable-goods industries, such as autos and machinery, and some services, such as medical care. Concentrations of market powers also played a role, particularly in the later stages of the cycle when expansion was slow yet prices and wages continued to rise. All in all, it was a period in which a state just a shade below full employment was combined with considerable inflation, an example of the unemployment-inflation dilemma at its worst.

Monetary policy took up much of the burden of fighting inflation. The Federal Reserve tightened credit, though only after a considerable time lag. No discretionary tax changes were made, expenditures rose slowly, and the budget moved into substantial surplus. Thus, although virtually no explicit discretionary fiscal measures were undertaken, the automatic stabilizers, particularly rising tax revenues, gradually gave the budget an anti-inflationary impact. The peculiar nature of the inflation, its concentration in a few sectors, and its cost-push element made this inflation particularly intractable to general fiscal (or monetary) policies.

What about the use of fiscal policy against future inflations? So far, inflations have had the disconcerting tendency of not following former patterns. One might be tempted to consider the inflation of the mid-fifties as a portent of future episodes. But since then, world industrial markets have become more integrated, and imports have added an important new competitive element to many domestic markets. The precise form of future inflations is impossible to predict, and the design of policies must await their diagnosis.

The price stability of the late fifties and early sixties was purchased at the cost of substantial unemployment. It remains to be seen, when full employment is restored, whether we have escaped from the unemployment-inflation dilemma. In any event, conventional fiscal policy cannot extricate us from that dilemma, and it would be unrealistic to expect it to do so.

Suggestions on Improving Fiscal Policy

On the whole, we have reason to be satisfied with counter-cyclical fiscal policy. The automatic stabilizers moderate swings in the economy. Discretionary action, while slower, limited in magnitude, and somewhat tardy, does make a significant contribution; and in the event of a larger and more prolonged downswing, it could be made more effective. If unemployment approached depression conditions, the political obstacles to the use of tax instruments would probably be overcome and there would be time for new expenditure programs to be started and for their effects to be felt.

Nevertheless, there is no reason for complacency. The recessions have been a serious matter, producing considerable unemployment and loss of output, and renewing deep-seated fears that they would become depressions. To strengthen our defenses against depression and to moderate further the more minor disturbances, two proposals have been advanced to make the automatic stabilizers even more powerful.

IMPROVED UNEMPLOYMENT BENEFITS

Under the present system, unemployment benefits offset only one-fifth to one-third of the decline in payrolls during a recession. Maximum benefits are rarely as much as one-half of average wages; a week or two usually has to pass before a worker is eligible to receive benefits; and the maximum benefit period varies from 13 to 26 weeks, yet as many as one-quarter of the unemployed may have been without jobs for more than 6 months. If unemployment benefits could offset more of the recession-induced payroll declines, this most sensitive and appropriate of automatic stabilizers would become more effective.

Proposals to improve the benefits have been made repeatedly. After some months of the 1958 and 1961 recessions, Congress authorized the states to extend the period of eligibility by 50 per cent, and lent them the money to do so. More permanent improvements of the system have foundered on the issue of federal control. Although the federal government pays the administrative cost in full, the states determine standards of eligibility, of benefit levels, and of duration. Past proposals have usually involved the setting of federal minimum standards. Perhaps in the future a formula will be found which will make the system more effective without imposing federal control. Since economic stabilization is a national responsibility, it might perhaps be appropriate to have the federal government underwrite recession-induced deficits of state unemployment insurance systems.

VARIABLE TAX RATES

The stability of the economy could be significantly enhanced by making personal income tax rates automatically variable. Rates would be changed, say, in response to an increase in the unemployment rate. Suppose that tax collections were cut by 5 per cent for every 1 per cent of unemployment in excess of 5 per cent. This is what would have happened in the recession year of 1958: Unemployment averaged 6.8 per cent, so taxes would have been reduced by 9 per cent (1.8 × 5), cutting revenues by an extra $4 billion. This would have raised automatic stabilization from $12 to $16 billion, or from 40 per cent to 53 per cent of the decline in GNP. This is a significant change. In comparison, a 50 per cent improvement in unemployment benefits would improve automatic stabilization by only $1 billion. Thus variable tax rates are a most powerful potential tool.

However, complete automaticity is difficult to accomplish because it places too heavy a burden on purely statistical indicators. If the tax rate change is to be tied to unemployment, one would wish to have a fool-proof system of unemployment statistics, perfectly adjusted for seasonal and frictional factors, and immune from erratic variations. There would also be some administrative problems in varying income tax collections within the year, since it is an annual tax. These difficulties could probably be overcome. But we are understandably reluctant to turn over the management of our fiscal affairs to a wholly mechanical procedure based on inevitably imperfect statistical data.

An alternative to complete automaticity is to give the president stand-by authority to change tax rates when economic conditions warrant. This would eliminate the need to go to the Congress and to face a political struggle over the details of tax changes when recession or inflation actually strikes, and thus might restore the tax instrument to the stabilization arsenal. The Congress would specify, in permanent legislation, under what unemployment and inflation conditions the president would be free to use this power, and would also specify the precise tax changes that could be made. This proposal was most recently advanced in the Report of the influential Commission on Money and Credit (1961). President Kennedy followed the commission's recommendation and requested such stand-by authority. However, the Congress was unreceptive to the idea, being most jealous of any infringement of its power of the purse.

Summary

The theory of fiscal policy is a corollary of national income analysis.

It views government expenditures as an addition to effective demand, taxes a reduction of effective demand. Modern fiscal policy requires that government expenditures and taxes be changed to achieve the stabilization objectives of full employment and stable prices. At times this requires that fiscal policy be expansionary (to raise expenditures and reduce taxes), and at other times to be restrictive (to reduce expenditures and increase taxes). The magnitudes of tax and expenditure changes required to accomplish any particular change in effective demand depend on the multiplier.

A balanced increase in the level of the budget, with both taxes and expenditures rising by the same amount, will normally raise the level of GNP, because part of the taxes will have come out of savings, while all the expenditures are spent.

In analyzing the historical record of budget deficits and surpluses, automatic changes must be distinguished from discretionary changes. Automatic changes are the result of movements in the private economy. When the economy enters recession, tax bases automatically shrink, yielding less revenue, and some categories of expenditures, such as unemployment benefits, automatically increase. Discretionary changes, on the other hand, are the result of explicit government action, such as changes in the tax rates or the institution of new spending programs. The concept of the full employment budget surplus permits the identification of changes in discretionary policy.

The actual management of fiscal policy requires more than a mechanical application of the theory. In each situation, certain complications and qualifications to the theory must be kept in mind.

Not all expenditures have the same multiplier effects. Transfer payments must be distinguished from purchases of goods and services since they do not constitute a direct demand in the initial round of the multiplier process. Not all households have the same marginal propensity to consume, and therefore the multiplier will differ, depending on the spending propensities of the recipients. Some expenditures go for imports and hence have no domestic multiplier. Some expenditures displace private expenditures rather than add to them.

Similarly, not all tax changes have the same multiplier effects. In some instances, the effect on business liquidity and investment is more important than the effect on consumption. Temporary tax changes may also have effects different from permanent tax changes.

The financing of budget deficits can have a restrictive effect, partly offsetting the benefits of an expansionary policy. If monetary policy is not sufficiently eased to permit both private and public borrowers to obtain funds at moderate interest cost, the government borrowing will compete with private borrowing, cutting private investment.

There are also practical difficulties in the use of fiscal policy. Discretionary policy runs into the serious time lags of recognition, decision, and of expenditure effects. Forecasting errors may also reduce its effectiveness.

If the economy has an inflationary bias, so that it is unable to support full employment without rising prices, fiscal policy cannot meet all the objectives of policy simultaneously. It must promote either price stability or full employment; it cannot promote both.

The annually balanced budget still receives much public support. If rigorously pursued, it would lead to disastrous results for the economy. It does, however, provide some damper on government spending, whereas the strictly counter-cyclical principles of modern fiscal policy do not contain any simple public yardstick that could discipline spending decisions arising out of the political process. The CED proposal of a slightly overbalanced budget at full employment attempts to combine the advantages of modern counter-cyclical policy with fiscal discipline.

Post-war fiscal policy has helped significantly to stabilize the economy. Deficits and surpluses have moved in a counter-cyclical manner, keeping the declines in total private purchasing power about one-half as large as the declines in total GNP.

Much the larger part of this maintenance of private purchasing power resulted from the workings of the automatic stabilizers. Discretionary policy made a minor contribution to stability. Post-war recessions, however, were brief and mild, and in the event of a more serious decline, discretionary policy could play a larger role.

Fiscal policy against inflation was used most extensively during the Korean War, when it was the main instrument of stabilization policy and tax rates were increased substantially. It did not prevent a largely psychological inflation, but moderated it. During the inflation after World War II, pent-up demands were so great that even a fiscal policy of budget surpluses could do no more than hasten the end of the inflation. The inflation of the mid-fifties was chiefly fought with monetary policy.

Fiscal policy could be made even more effective if the unemployment insurance system were strengthened, and if tax rates were made either automatically variable or else variable at the president's discretion.

8

THE ECONOMICS OF THE PUBLIC DEBT

When revenues fall short of expenditures, governments borrow. This process has left most governments with large outstanding debts. Interest has to be paid on these debts by the taxpayers, and when the bonds expire, they have to be repaid or refinanced through new borrowing.

The sheer size of the federal government's debt poses severe problems for our Treasury. On the one hand, the Treasury must preserve the credit of the government by successfully refinancing the maturing bond issues and meeting any new deficits, all at reasonable interest cost. On the other hand, the national debt is of such magnitude that its management affects the performance of the economy. Thus, as in the case of fiscal policy, the government must consider its own immediate financial problems, yet also consider its effects on the performance of the economy as a whole.

In this brief chapter, we consider two questions. First, what is the burden of the debt and what has happened to it over time? Second, viewing debt management as an instrument of economic policy, how can it make a contribution to the achievement of economic stability?

Growth of Debt

Figure 16 shows the growth of the national public debt since World War I. About one-third of the $25 billion borrowed in World War I was repaid in the 1920's. The years of the Great Depression saw the debt increase from $16 billion to $40 billion. But most of the debt was acquired during World War II, at the end of which it had reached $259 billion. Thereafter, it stayed level until 1957, with surpluses occurring in some years of prosperity and deficits occurring in recession and in some of the Korean War years. Since 1957 the debt has increased, from $270 billion to over $300 billion by 1964. The increase in the debt is largely due to war, and secondarily to periods of unemployment when the response to economic conditions—falling revenues and rising expenditures—has put the budget into deficit.

The figure $300 billion is high—$1,600 for every man, woman, and child in the United States. But to interpret this figure it must be put into some perspective. Figure 17 shows the ratio of the national debt to GNP, which, in a general way, is the tax base out of which the interest cost must be met. This ratio has fallen steadily since its World War II peak. In 1946 the debt was

FIG. 16   The federal debt.

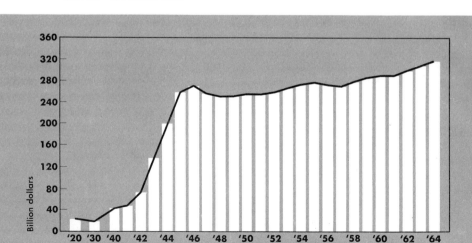

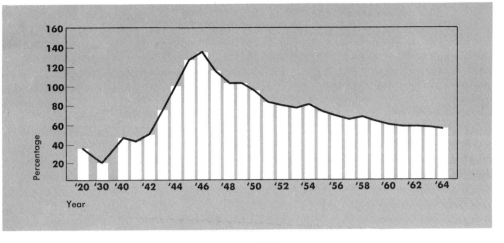

FIG. 17 Federal debt as a percentage of GNP.

130 per cent of GNP; in 1963 it had fallen to 60 per cent. This decline was due, in roughly equal parts, to a growth of real output (up 73 per cent), and the rise in the price level (up 59 per cent). We can take satisfaction in the reduction of the relative burden of the debt due to the growth of output; but the decline of the real burden caused by repeated inflations, a factor of almost equal importance, means only that the holders of the debt have seen the real value of their bonds eroded.

The national debt must also be seen in relation to the total debt in the economy. Figure 18 shows that since World War II private debt, particularly for home mortgages, consumer credit, and business borrowing, has increased much more rapidly. In 1946 private debt was somewhat less than the national debt; by 1964 it was more than twice as great. In the public sector, state and local debt increased enormously.

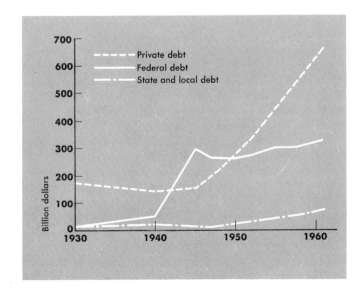

FIG. 18 National debt in relation to total debt.

Another relevant dimension of the debt is the volume of interest payments. This is a payment which has to be made by the taxpayers every year and depends not only on the size of the debt but also on the average interest rate. Figure 19 shows both the absolute interest payments on the national debt as well as their relationship to GNP. Interest payments have increased considerably more than the debt itself, because interest rates have been on a rising trend through much of this period. As the older low-interest securities have had to be refinanced, the government has had to pay substantially higher interest rates.

WHAT IS THE BURDEN OF THE DEBT?

With a national debt of $1,600 per capita, it is only natural that it occupy the minds of politicians, editorial writers, citizens, and economists. Intuition tells us we would be better off wthout the debt, just as we would wish to be free of personal debts. Yet to sort out the real burdens from the fancied requires the most careful economic analysis, and it is in fact one of the slipperiest problems to confront the economic theorist.

FIG. 19   Federal interest payments and federal interest payments as a percentage of GNP.

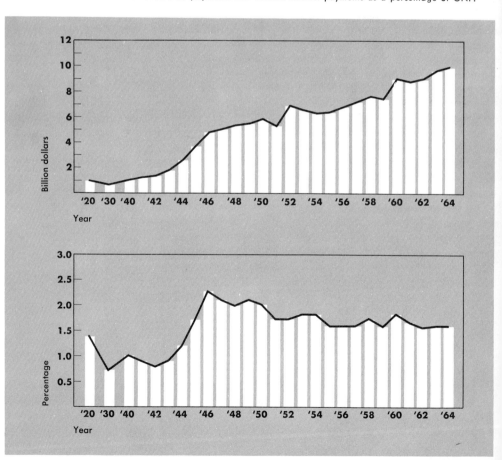

To define the burden of the debt precisely, we have to ask this question: What difference does it make to us and to future generations that certain past government expenditures were financed by borrowing rather than by taxation? For if they had been financed out of taxation, there would now be no debt and there could be no "burden" of that debt.

THE BURDEN IN TERMS OF REAL RESOURCES

Two-thirds of our national debt was acquired during World War II. The tangible burden of that war certainly does not rest on our shoulders today. The lives lost and the material resources required to win it were expended in the war years; no financial arrangement can change that simple fact. Even though a large national debt was incurred in the years 1942 to 1945, future generations are not being asked to fight the war. Thus, the real cost of past war expenditures has already been incurred.

What about debt incurred during periods of unemployment? In this case the real burden of deficit-financed expenditures is limited even at the time expenditures are made. Resources would have been idle, so no other outputs are foregone. In fact, output is likely to be increased by the multiplier effects of the initial spending. Thus, the creation of debt in this situation raises output, and is likely to raise investment and the total growth of the economy.

EXTERNAL VERSUS INTERNAL DEBT

When an underdeveloped country borrows abroad to build a dam, or when a town issues bonds for some public work, it acquires an external debt which has to be repaid at some future date. Just as in the case of an individual, the borrowing increases the total resources available initially, but reduces the resources available in the future. To meet the interest and repayment charges owed to the outside world, the government must reduce future public spending or raise taxes and reduce private spending, thus cutting total internal resource use. In effect, the borrowing simply makes the resources available earlier in exchange for the interest payments. The initial increase in total available resources is made possible by borrowing done outside the community. Similarly, interest and repayment means that the community gives up resources to the outside world.

When our national government borrows, the process is not the same, because the borrowing occurs within the country, so that the total resources available to the country as a whole are not increased. The resources are simply transferred from the bond-buyers to the government, which expends them for public purposes. Similarly, the interest and repayment charges do not transfer resources outside the country as a whole but only transfer them from the taxpayers to the bond-holders. This distinction between an external and an internal debt is fundamental. An internally held debt represents only a commitment to effect a certain transfer of purchasing power among the individuals within the country. It does not commit the country to give up real output to another country.

Thus, when it comes to the national debt, there is a fundamental truth in the phrase, "We owe it to ourselves," although, as we shall see in a moment, "we" is not always the same individuals and there are some harmful side-effects which are a real burden.

One burden of a public debt is unambiguous. Extra taxes have to be imposed to finance the interest payments. They lead to some loss of real output because of their distorting and disincentive effects. Even though the redistribution of income from the taxpayers to the interest recipients is only a transfer payment, it does contribute to the negative effects of the tax system we discussed at length in Chapter 6. This deadweight loss is borne year after year as the interest payments continue to be met. Had the debt not been incurred earlier, this loss would not be suffered; hence it is a genuine burden of the debt.[1]

LOSS OF OUTPUT: REDUCED INVESTMENT?

If debt financing leads to a decline in investment, there will be another unambiguous loss of output. Future generations then inherit a smaller stock of capital, an economy with a smaller capacity to produce, hence a smaller output. For example, during World War II net investment was extremely small as resources were heavily diverted to military needs. In fact, the allocation of resources in World War II was largely determined by various direct controls; private saving was very large, yet private investment was kept small because the materials could not be spared for building private plants and equipment. Thus the World War II debt cannot be said to have cut investment. Perhaps other deficits did have negative effects on the private capital stock, though in the case of recession and depression, one would expect the general stimulating effects of the deficit to raise rather than to cut investment. In general, if the government could accomplish its objectives by selling fewer bonds to the public, interest rates might be lower, funds for private investment more readily available, and some additional private investment might be undertaken.

Investment may also be reduced by the presence of an existing public debt. Certainly, the higher taxes must have some negative influence on investment, although this factor has to be weighed against the high savings propensities of the interest recipients. Also, the existence of the large debt may have psychological influences on business behavior. If people really get alarmed over the national debt, they might curtail their investments. The significance of this psychological factor is difficult to evaluate.

DOES THE DEBT SHIFT THE BURDEN
OF PAST EXPENDITURES INTO THE FUTURE?

Apart from output effects which clearly make future generations worse off, is it possible to shift the burden of past expenditures into the future? For a long time economists thought that it was impossible. An internal debt does not shift the availability and use of resources through time and hence can do no more than reshuffle incomes within future generations. But about 1958, several economists began to develop doubts whether this was the complete analysis.[2] They asked themselves this question. Under bond-financing of a

---

[1] But think of the tax distortions that would have been caused in the war years if the entire war costs had been met by taxes. Half of all incomes would have had to be taken in taxes. The economy would hardly have been able to function—then how would the war have been won?

[2] J. M. Buchanan, *Public Principles of Public Debt* (Homewood, Ill.: Irwin, 1958), and W. G. Bowen, R. G. Davis, and D. H. Kopf, "The Public Debt," *American Economic Review,* Vol. L (September, 1960), pp. 701-705.

war, which individuals of the wartime generation actually bear the burden? Under tax-financing the issue is clear; the wartime taxpayers have to reduce their consumption, and thereby release resources for war. Under bond-financing, the bond-buyers also reduce their consumption, but in exchange they obtain a bond which entitles them to increase their consumption at a later date. Thus they lend to the society the resources to fight the war; but in exchange they obtain a claim to receive interest which they are free to consume, whereas if they had paid only taxes they would receive nothing. Should they wish, they can sell the bonds and consume the proceeds at any time.

Thus, if the individuals of the society can be neatly divided into the wartime bond-buyers and post-war taxpayers—a rather arbitrary grouping— and if they then can be identified as "generations," it is in fact possible to shift some of the burden of the war to a future generation, by giving the wartime generation a claim against the income of future taxpayers. Thus the long acknowledged income redistribution from taxpayers to bond-holders has been identified as a redistribution among generations, a shifting of the burden to the future. (Only some of the burden can be so shifted, because the full cost of the war consists of far more than the expenditure of money. The lost lives, the hardships suffered by the troops, the separation of families, the shortages of civilian goods—all these occur regardless of the method of financing.)

It is not clear that the resultant income redistribution is significant as an empirical matter or as a matter of social policy. Bond-ownership and tax payments are not distributed so very differently, so that even in this individual sense there is a certain amount of "I owe it to myself." Nor can the groups so clearly be identified by age and hence by generations. It is certainly not true that the older generation owns all the bonds and the younger generation pays the taxes. Furthermore, the bonds may be passed on as inheritance, just as tax liabilities continue.

Does this resultant income redistribution really constitute a shifting of the burden of earlier expenditures to the future? If you think only of the real resources, it does not, because the war has still been fought by the older generation and the resources withdrawn from the private economy during that time. Nor is there any change in the output available in the future, leaving aside the minor output effects. But in an individual sense, there is some shifting of the burden since future generations are required to pay interest to the people who acquired the bonds during the war and to their inheritors. Had the older generation been forced to pay taxes instead, this compulsory redistribution would not occur at the later date.

The Structure of the Debt and Debt Management Policy

The debt is held by various financial institutions, individuals, and state and local governments. Table 13 summarizes the distribution of the ownership of the federal debt, as well as the changes since 1946. The public mostly holds savings bonds, long-term securities which cannot be sold in the market but which can be redeemed at the Treasury at a fixed schedule at any time. Savings bonds represent $48 billion of the total debt. Most of the rest consists of marketable securities which fluctuate with the interest rates in the economy.[3] (Savings bonds were made non-marketable in order to free the ordinary saver from the risks of fluctuations in the capital value of the bonds caused by interest rate changes.)

Commercial banks, insurance companies, and savings banks reduced their government-bond holdings in the post-war period as they found better-

TABLE 13

Ownership of U.S. Government Securities
(Billions of dollars—end of fiscal year)

	Total	U.S. Govt. Accounts	Federal Reserve System	Commercial Banks	Insurance Companies	Mutual Savings Banks	Corporations	Individuals	State and Local	Other (foreign, etc.)
1946	270	29	24	84	25	12	18	63	6	9
1963	306	57	31	63	11	6	22	66	21	28
Net Change 1946-1963	+36	+28	+7	−21	−14	−6	+4	+3	+15	+19

yielding alternative investments, particularly in the private sector. The major purchasers of the debt have been state and local governments, federal trust funds (social security, etc.), and foreigners, especially foreign central banks.

The $300 billion national debt requires continuous management as old issues expire and as budget deficits or surpluses cause the debt to change. The Treasury fights a never-ending battle to keep the average length of the debt from getting shorter and shorter as time passes and all outstanding securities move closer to their maturity date (see Fig. 20). (The length of the debt is defined as the average period for all securities before they fall due.) The average length has fallen in most years. By 1963, $85 billion were coming due in the succeeding 12 months, $143 billion within 5 years, and the rest scattered all the way to 1999.

A Policy Dilemma

Facing enormous financing needs and severe competition from private borrowers offering higher interest rates, the Treasury faces difficult decisions of debt management policy every few months when it has to decide the terms of its new security issues. Private companies, particularly heavy borrowers such as the American Telephone and Telegraph Company, face similar situations. But the Treasury's problems are complicated by one important additional consideration. It must not only concern itself with low-cost financing, but also must consider the interests of the economy as a whole, particularly the needs of stabilization policy. If the Treasury followed the same policy as a private company, seeking only to minimize its interest costs, it would issue vast quantities of long-term bonds at the bottom of a recession when long-term funds are ample and interest rates are lowest. It would issue only short-term securities in high-interest boom times.

[3] A total of $55 billion of the bonds, including some tailor-made issues, are held by the trust funds of the federal government itself. The Federal Reserve System holds another $31 billion. Thus, the debt held by the public is only $220 billion.

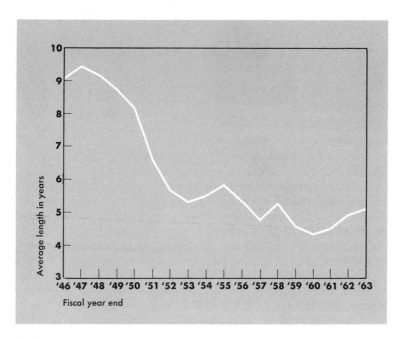

FIG. 20 Average length of debt.

But this policy would increase the instability of the economy. Government issues of long-term bonds in recession compete with private investment, making capital more scarce and raising interest rates. During inflation, proper stabilization policy requires that the Treasury issue long-term securities to help reduce the amount of credit available to private investors; yet such a policy would make the interest cost of the debt particularly high. Thus there is an inevitable conflict between the two objectives of low interest cost to minimize the burden to the taxpayers, and economic stabilization.

In practice, this conflict has been pretty much resolved in favor of low interest costs. Virtually all the long-term bonds have been sold in periods when interest rates were low, when there was considerable unemployment. Figure 20 shows that most of the debt-lengthening occurred in recession years. The Treasury felt that the difficulties and the costs of selling bonds during booms were prohibitive.

The Treasury has sought to make a virtue out of this necessity by adopting a permanent policy of lengthening the maturity structure. With its frequent refinancing, the debt has seriously interfered with a proper counter-cyclical monetary policy. Whenever the Treasury is selling bonds, the Federal Reserve must be particularly careful that the capital market will not tighten; otherwise the Treasury will fail to sell its new issue and government credit will be impaired. If the Treasury has to go to market to raise money too often, the number of weeks in the year in which the Federal Reserve is prevented from applying a restrictive monetary policy becomes a substantial fraction of all the weeks. Thus one of the objectives of debt management has been to reduce the number of Treasury trips to market by putting more of the debt into long-term form. The Treasury reasons that its sales of long-term securities in recession improve the stability of the economy by making it possible to conduct a more flexible monetary policy during all phases of the business cycle in the future, while, hopefully, long-term credit will be kept ample in recession even in the face of the Treasury's actions. At the same time, a longer-term debt structure reduces the pressure on the Treasury to find funds. This makes the refinancing task easier and should lead eventually to lower interest costs.

Recent Improvements in Debt Management Technique

Confronted by the recurrent difficulty of refinancing the debt, particularly in prosperous periods, the Treasury has adopted several new marketing techniques. The most important of these is *advance refunding*. Under this technique, holders of bonds which are to expire within a few years are given an opportunity to exchange them for new bonds on rather favorable terms. The Treasury's aim is to keep its long-time bond-holders from switching into other securities when its issues reach maturity. Advance refunding has been very effective. It has enabled the Treasury to refinance over $40 billion of government bonds from 1959 to 1963, without upsetting the general capital market, and has made possible a major lengthening of the average maturity of the debt. The technique bypasses the open capital market, and thus probably reduces the government's competition with private long-term issues.

The Treasury has also experimented with the *auctioning* of bonds to private underwriting syndicates. Traditionally, the Treasury has sold its bonds by announcing the interest and maturity terms of a new issue, and inviting subscription offers. The Treasury has to make the terms sufficiently attractive so that enough of each issue is bought to preserve the credit of the government. In periods of rising interest rates, the risk of an issue's failing is great, and this is one of the main reasons why the Treasury has been forced to confine its long-term financing to recession periods. In an auction, the standard technique of private industry, no fixed price is attached to the issue but competitive bids are invited, and the underwriting syndicate which offers the best terms gets to buy the bonds and market them. Since 1962 the Treasury has experimented with this technique, so far with only mixed success and only with small issues.

Summary

America's national debt is now over $300 billion, or $1,600 for every man, woman, and child in the country. Most of this debt was incurred during war, most of the remainder was due to budget deficits in periods of unemployment. Although the debt is very large, it has been shrinking in relation to GNP partly because of real growth of output, partly because the rise in the price level has reduced the real value of the debt. The federal debt has also become a smaller part of the total debt in the economy, as private and state and local borrowing have risen rapidly through most of the post-war period.

The burden of a public debt is not analogous to that of a private debt. If the debt is internal to the country, interest payments and future retirement of the debt do not require that resources be transferred outside the country. Thus, except for some relatively minor side-effects, the total goods and services available to the economy remain unchanged.

One clear burden of a public debt is any reduction in output which its existence causes. To the extent that the taxes necessary to meet the interest payments have disincentive effects and cause a misallocation of resources, the debt does reduce output. If the debt also reduces investment, the future inherits a smaller capital stock and hence less potential output.

Can one generation shift the burden of the costs of its expenditures to a future generation by borrowing? Can the burden of a war be transferred to the future? In one sense, yes; in another, no. The real resources have to be expended at the time the war is fought. However, the wartime generation which chose to borrow rather than to tax itself can collect interest on its bonds from future taxpayers. It can also cash in its bonds and consume the proceeds. Thus, debt-financing of a war rather than tax-financing gives the wartime generation a future claim against the income of taxpayers.

The structure of the debt ranges from 90-day bills to bonds not due until the end of the century. There has been a tendency for the debt to shorten its average maturity as the Treasury has found it difficult to sell a sufficient number of long-term bonds.

The management of the federal debt poses a conflict between two objectives. On the one hand, interest cost should be minimized. On the other hand, the effect on the performance of the economy should be considered. Minimum interest cost requires that the debt be lengthened in recession, when long-term interest rates are low. Economic stabilization requires the opposite, that the debt be lengthened in booms, when borrowing should be made more difficult for private investors. This dilemma has in practice been largely resolved in favor of minimizing interest costs.

In order to improve the marketability of the debt, the Treasury has made several innovations in the last few years. The technique of advance refunding gives the holders of old bonds the opportunity to exchange them for new bonds on favorable terms before their maturity date. This is an attempt by the Treasury to retain its traditional customers. It has also experimented with the auctioning techniques used by private enterprise, inviting private underwriting syndicates to bid on Treasury issues. So far this experiment has had only mixed success.

For more elaborate general treatments of public finance, see any of the good intermediate-level textbooks, as for example, John F. Due, *Government Finance,* 3rd. ed. (Homewood, Ill.: Irwin, 1963); Harold M. Groves, *Financing Government,* 5th. ed. (New York Holt, 1958); Earl R. Rolph and George F. Break, *Public Finance* (New York: Ronald, 1961); and William J. Shultz and C. Lowell Harriss, *American Public Finance,* 6th. ed. (Englewood Cliffs, N.J.: Prentice-Hall, 1954).

For a full and authoritative account of the theoretical aspects of public finance see Richard A. Musgrave, *The Theory of Public Finance* (New York: McGraw-Hill, 1959). This is an advanced and difficult treatise.

On the proper scope of government, see the papers by Walter Heller and Frazer B. Wilde in the volume *Federal Expenditure Policy for Economic Growth and Stability* (Joint Economic Committee, U.S. Congress, 1957). John K. Galbraith's famous *The Affluent Society* (New York: Houghton Mifflin, 1958) presents the argument that the quality of public services in the U.S. is too low.

The best book on promoting efficiency in the public sector is Charles J. Hitch and Roland N. McKean, *The Economics of Defense in the Nuclear Age* (Cambridge: Harvard University Press, 1960). Interesting papers on the economics of expenditures can also be found in National Bureau of Economic Research, *Public Finances: Needs, Sources and Utilization* (Princeton: Princeton University Press, 1960), and in the Joint Economic Committee volume mentioned above. The single most informative source is the *Budget of the United States Government* which appears annually and neatly summarizes the president's expenditure policies, both in the aggregate and for each program. Two good books on budgeting are Jesse Burkhead, *Government Budgeting* (New York: Wiley, 1957); and Arthur Smithies, *The Budgetary Process in the United States* (New York: McGraw-Hill, 1955).

On the problems of state and local governments see papers by Dick Netzer, L. L. Ecker-Racz, and I. M. Labovitz in the volume *Public Finances: Needs, Sources and Utilization* (see above); also papers by Groves, Stigler, Maxwell, and Buchanan in the Joint Economic Committee volume *Federal Expenditure Policy* (see above).

On metropolitan areas see the book of readings, *Economics of Metropolitan Areas,* edited by Benjamin Chinitz (Englewood Cliffs, N.J.: Prentice-Hall, 1964).

The literature on the economics of taxation is enormous. On questions of equity, the fundamental source remains Henry C. Simons, *Personal Income Taxation* (Chicago: University of Chicago Press, 1938). Contemporary views on issues of tax policy can be found in Dan Throop Smith, *Federal Tax Reform* (New York: McGraw-Hill, 1961); and the three-volume *Tax Revision Compendium* published by the House Ways and Means Committee, U.S. Congress, 1959. Also see the *President's 1963 Tax Message* published by the House Ways and Means Committee. The most comprehensive study of the effects of the tax system on economic efficiency and growth was undertaken at the Harvard Graduate School of Business Administration around 1950 and published in the series *Effects of Taxation.* One of the most interesting studies was J. K. Butters, L. E. Thompson, and L. L. Bollinger, *Effects of Taxation: Investment by Individuals* (Boston: Harvard University Graduate School of Business Administration, 1953).

Wilfred Lewis, Jr.'s *Federal Fiscal Policy in the Postwar Recessions* (Washington, D.C.: The Brookings Institution, 1962), is a good introduction to fiscal policy in practice. Also see Arthur F. Burns, *Prosperity without Inflation* (New York: Fordham University Press, 1957); and *Staff Report on Employment, Growth and Price Levels,* Joint Economic Committee, U.S. Congress, 1959.

For discussion of the burden of the debt, see the works cited in Chapter 8, and replies in later issues of the *American Economic Review.* On problems of debt management see W. L. Smith, *Debt Management in the United States,* Study Paper No. 19, Joint Economic Committee, U.S. Congress, 1960.

INDEX

Ability-to-pay principle, 55, 69
Acceptability, 54, 69
Administrative Budget, 23, 31
Adjusted gross income, 57, 61
Advance refunding, 114, 115
Advisory Commission on Intergovernmental Relations: *Alternative Approaches to Governmental Reorganization in Metropolitan Areas*, 49; *Factors Affecting Voter Reactions to Governmental Reorganization in Metropolitan Areas*, 49; *Measures of State and Local Fiscal Capacity and Tax Effort*, 38
Agriculture expenditures, 5
Albuquerque, New Mexico, 48
Alcoholic beverage taxes, by state, 40-41
American Telephone and Telegraph Co., 17, 112
Annually balanced budget, 95-97, 104
Appropriation, 21
Appropriation Committees, 21, 22
Arkansas River, 14
Atomic energy, 16
Auctioning of bonds, 114, 115
Automatic stabilizers, 89, 98, 101, 104
Automatic *vs.* discretionary changes, 88-90, 103
Averaging of income, 65-66
Average effective tax rates, 60, 73

Backdoor financing, 21n
Ballots *vs.* markets, 17-19
Bargaining in budget cycle, 31
Benefits and costs: principle of equating at margin, 23-26, 32; private *vs.* social, 11
Benefit principle of taxation, 53, 69; applied to corporation income tax, 68; highways, 53; special assessments, 55
Benson, George C. S., *Consolidated Grants: A Means of Maintaining Fiscal Responsibility*, 39
Block grants, 39; in Canada, 42
Bollinger, L. L., *Effects of Taxation on Investment by Individuals*, 79-80, 116
Boston, Massachusetts, 49
Brazer, Harvey, 2
Break, George F., 74; *Public Finance*, 116
Budget, 21-23, 31; as decision-making process, 21-22; balanced change, 86-87, 103; concepts, 22-23, 31; deficits and surpluses, 87-89, 104; effect on demand, 84-104; full employment surplus, 88
Budget of the United States Government, 22, 116
Budget on National Income and Product Account, 23, 31
Budget principles, 87, 95-98
Burden of public debt, 109-111
Bureau of the Budget, 21, 31
Bureau of Reclamation, 28
Burkhead, Jesse, *Government Budgeting*, 116
Burns, Arthur F., *Prosperity without Inflation*, 116
Butters, J. K., *Effects of Taxation on Investment by Individuals*, 79-80, 116

Canada, block grant system, 42
Capital gains, 61n, 75; effect of lower rates on personal investment, 80; tax treatment, 63-64
Capitalism, 16, 19
Charitable contributions, 54
Chinitz, Benjamin (ed.), *Economics of Metropolitan Areas*, 116
Cleveland, Ohio, 48
Cohn, Samuel M., 2
Collection costs, 54, 69
Collective goods: *defined*, 11; national *vs.* local, 36
Commission on Intergovernmental Relations, *A Report to the President*, 39, 42
Commission on Money and Credit, 103
Committee for Economic Development, 97-98; CED Plan, 97-98, 104
Communications satellite, 17
Compliance costs, 54, 69
Conditional grants, 42
Congestion, and pricing of highway services, 28
Congress, 10, 21, 22, 31, 39, 66, 67, 94, 103
Consolidated Cash Budget, 5, 23, 31
Consolidated grants, 39
Consumption: effects of excise taxes, 71-72; effects of government expenditures, 86-87, 92; effects of public debt, 111; effects of taxation, 85-87
Consumption function, 85-86, 92
Coordination, in metropolitan areas, 46, 50
Core city, 45, 46, 50
Corporation income tax: and economic growth, 75-80; as automatic stabilizer, 89, 98; depreciation, 77-79; double taxation, 67, 69; effect on growing enterprises, 76-77; effect on rate of return, 75-76; effect on supply of investible funds, 76-77, 83; in states, 40-41; multiplier effects, 92-93; preferential treatment, 67, 69; shifting, 68, 76; structure, 75
Corps of Engineers, 28
Cost-plus contracts, 30

David, Martin, 2
Dead-weight loss, 71-72
Debt management, 111-115
Decentralization, 35
Decision lag, 93
Decision-making: ballots *vs.* markets, 17; distortions due to taxation, 71; improvements in government, 28; in metropolitan areas, 45; local *vs.* central government, 34; rational design of process, 28-30, 32
Deductions: enforceability, 54; under federal income tax, 58-62, 69
Defense: a collective good, 11; and benefit-cost principle, 25; expenditures, 5
Deficits, 88; financing, 93, 104
Department of Defense: budget program by purpose, 29; commercial activities, 16; improvements in decision-making process, 28-32; incentive contracts, 30
Depletion allowance, 67
Depreciation: methods, 77-78; tax treatment of, 77-79, 83
Depression, as cause of government intervention, 13
Dividend credit, 68
Dividend exclusion, 68
Discretionary policies, 89, 103-104; distinguished from automatic, 88-90; forecasting

117

errors, 94; in 1958 recession, 100-101; time lags, 93-94
Displacement effect, 10
Distribution of income, 2
Doing-business tax, 68
Dorfman, R., *Price Theory*, 27n
Double taxation, 67-69
Due, John F., *Government Finance*, 116

Earmarking, 22, 55
Ecker-Racz, L. L., 116
Eckstein, Otto, *Multiple Purpose River Development*, 12
Economic growth: of demand *vs.* supply, 82; tax system and, 75-83
Economic life, 77
Economies of scale, in public services, 47-48, 50
Education: and benefit-cost principle, 25; advantage of local control, 35; and national interest, 36; economies of scale, 47; expenditures, 5, 38, 40; in metropolitan areas, 44; private *vs.* social benefits, 13
Efficiency: in government, 20-32; in metropolitan areas, 45-48; tax system and, 70-75, 83
Eisenhower, Dwight, D., 10, 39, 110
Electric power: and benefit-cost principle, 25; border area between private and public sectors, 16; physical interdependence illustrated, 12; private *vs.* public, 12, 16; TVA as producer, 14
Eminent domain, 13
Equalizing grants, 39
Equity: criteria defined, 54-56, 69; horizontal, 55, 69; vertical, 55, 69
Erosion of tax base, 61, 69, 75
Estate and gift taxes, 66; effect on small companies, 77n
Excess profits tax, 101
Excise taxes: discriminatory, 66, 69; distortions caused by, 71-72, 83; effect on growth of demand, 82; regressive, 57
Exclusions, 58-61, 69
Exclusion principle, 11
Exemptions, 59-62, 69
Expenditures (*see* Government expenditures)
Expenditure tax, 56, 81
External economies and diseconomies (*see also* Physical interdependence): *defined*, 11; in housing, 45; in metropolitan areas, 45
External *vs.* internal debt, 109

Federal Reserve System, 33, 42, 113; and financing deficits, 93; time lags, 94
Fiscal capacity of states, 38-39, 42
Fiscal policy: *defined*, 84; theory of, 85-90
Flexibility, and least-cost solutions, 27
Flood control: a collective good, 11; project analysis, 24-25
Forecasting errors, 25, 94, 104
Foreign aid: a collective good, 11
Foreign Relations Committee, 21
Forest service, 17
France: tax system, 52; use of depreciation allowances, 79n; value-added tax, 80
Friedman, M., *The Theory of the Consumption Function*, 92n
Full employment, 84-85; budget, 89-90, 103; conflict with price level stability, 94-95, 101

Galbraith, John K., *The Affluent Society*, 116
Gasoline taxes: as price of service, 28n; rates by state, 40-41
Gift taxes, 66
Gill, Richard T., 2
Government: as a source of initiative, 14; scope of, 3-19
Government bonds, 112-115
Government expenditures, 2; by function, 5-6; criteria for, 22-27; effects on demand, 85-92, 103; exhaustive, 4; growth of, 4-10; in recession of *1958*, 98-100; lags in, 93; multiplier effects, 84-87, 91-92; transfers, 4
Grants-in-aid, 4, 37-39; block, 39-42; conditional, 42; consolidated, 39; equalizing, 39; matching, 42
Grossman, Gregory, *Economic Systems*, 15n
Gross production tax, 41
Groves, Harold M., *Financing Government*, 116

Harriss, C. Lowell, *American Public Finance*, 116
Health expenditures, 5
Heller, Walter, 116
Highways: benefit principle applied, 55; federal program, 49, 50; growth of expenditures, 5, 34, 38; in metropolitan areas, 46; pricing of service, 27-28; toll roads, 49
Hitch, Charles J., *The Economics of Defense in the Nuclear Age*, 116
Homeownership, tax treatment of, 62-63
Hoover, Herbert, 95
Horizontal equity, 55-56, 69
Housing: expenditures, 5; government changing pattern of consumption, 14; slums, 45, 50
Hungry Horse Dam, 12

Imports, and multiplier, 91, 103
Incentive contracts, 30
Incidence of tax, 52
Income: adjusted gross, 61; as base of taxation, 52, 55-56; effects of fiscal policy on, 85-92; taxable, 60-61
Income-in-kind, exclusions under income tax, 57, 60-61
Income splitting, 62; not in England, 74
Income taxation (*see also* Corporation income taxation; Personal income tax; Redistribution of income): alternatives, 80; by states, 37-38, 40-41
Inflation: as cause of government intervention, 13; conflict with full employment, 95, 96, 101, 104; cost-push, 101; deficits and, 96; fiscal policy against, 84, 100-101, 104
Insurance, border area between private and public sector, 16
Intangibles, and least-cost solutions, 26
Interest cost of debt, 5, 108, 110
Interest rates, 111-112
Internal Revenue Service, 52, 54n
Investment credit, 79, 83
Investment: effect of corporation, 75-77; reduced by taxes, 86
Italy, 52

Kaldor, Nicholas, 56
Kennedy, John F., 103
Kestnbaum Commission (*see* Commission on Intergovernmental Relations)

Krutilla, J. V., *Multiple Purpose River Development*, 12n

Labovitz, I. M., 116
Lakewood Plan, 48, 50
Law of diminishing benefit, 24
Least-cost solutions, 26
Lewis, Wilfred, Jr., *Federal Fiscal Policy in the Postwar Recessions*, 99n, 116
Local government, advantages, 34-36, 42
Los Angeles Metropolitan Water District, 48
Loss, carry-back and carry-forward, 76
Louisville, Kentucky, 48

Marginal cost pricing, 27
Marginal propensity to consume, 86-87; differences among households, 91-92, 103; and multiplier, 86-87
Marginal tax rates, 73
Marx, Karl, 15
Mass transit: federal aid, 49; in metropolitan areas, 46
Massachusetts Metropolitan District Commission, 49
Matching grants, 42
McClelland, Harold F., *Consolidated Grants: A Means of Maintaining Fiscal Responsibility*, 39
McKean, Roland N., *The Economics of Defense in the Nuclear Age*, 116
Memphis, Tennessee, 48
Metropolitan areas: economic integration, 43-44; land use, 44; population, 44; transportation, 44
Metropolitan consolidation, 47; economies of scale, 47
Metropolitan Special Districts, 48-50
Miami, Florida, 48
Military Affairs Committee, 21
Military Air Transport Service, 17
Minuteman missiles, 28-29
Monopoly and inflation, 95 (*see also* Natural monopoly)
Multiplier, 86-87, 91-92, 103
Musgrave, R. A., *The Theory of Public Finance*, 57, 116

National debt (*see* Public debt)
National government, advantages, 36, 42
National interest, and choice of level of government, 36
Natural monopolies, and scope of government, 13, 19
Natural resources expenditures, 5
Navy, 28
Netzer, Dick, 116
Neutrality, 71, 79
New Deal, 7, 10, 19
New York Port Authority, 48

Outdoor recreation, 17

Parks, and pricing of service, 27
Parimutuel tax, 41
Peacock, Alan T., *The Growth of Public Expenditure in the United Kingdom*, 8-9
Pechman, Joseph A., 2
Pension plans, 64-65, 75
Personal income tax: by state, 40-41; effect on demand, 82, 85-92; effect on efficiency, 73-75, 83; effect on income distribution, 58; effect on saving, 79-80, 83; effect on small companies, 77n; effect on supply of effort, 73-75; issues of fairness, 61-66; marginal and average rates, 59-60, 73; rate structure of federal, 59-60
Physical interdependence (*see also* External economies): as source of divergence between private and social costs or benefits, 11-12; in metropolitan areas, 45-47, 50
Planning, in metropolitan areas, 45
Polaris submarines, 28-29
Police and fire protection: economies of scale, 47; expenditures, 5, 38-40; in metropolitan areas, 44
Political process, as choice mechanism, 18
Post Office, pricing of services, 27
Power (*see* Electric power)
President's 1963 Tax Message, 116
Pricing of public services, 27-28
Private good, *defined*, 11
Private sector, 3, 10, 19
Productivity, in government, 7
Property taxes, 57; certainty, 54; growth of revenues, 37-38
Public assistance (relief): expenditures, 5, 34, 38; federal grants, 48
Public debt, 2; burden of, 109-111; external *vs.* internal, 109; growth, 106-108; inflation and, 107; interest cost, 108, 110, 112; loss of output, 110; real resource burden, 109; tax costs, 110
Public Finances: Needs, Sources and Utilization, 116
Public sector, 3, 4, 10, 19
Public welfare (*see also* Public assistance): growth of expenditures, 34, 38
Public works, 94, 100

RAND Corporation, 27n
Raw fish tax (Alaska), 40
Recession of 1958, 98-99
Recognition lag, 93
Redistribution multiplier, 91
Redistribution of income, 14; and expenditures, 7, 15, 19; result of public debt, 11; result of taxation, 57-58
Requirements approach, 25-26
Revenues (*see* Taxation)
Risks and government intervention, 13
Rolph, Earl R., *Public Finance*, 116
Roosevelt, Franklin D., 95
Routes to full employment, 88
Russia, 15

St. Louis, Missouri, 47, 48
Sales taxes: by state, 40-41; growth of revenues, 37-38; multiplier effects, 92; proportionate and regressive, 57; proposed for federal government, 81, 83
Salt tax, 72
Sanders, T. H., *Effects of Taxation on Executives*, 73
Saving: effect of tax system, 79; expenditure tax and, 81
Savings bonds, 111-112
Schultze, Charles L., *National Income Analysis*, 92n

Scope of government, 2-10, 19; changed under New Deal, 8
Seattle Metropolitan Municipal Corporation, 48
Selective excise taxes, by state, 40-41
Severance taxes, 40-41
Sewers: economies of scale, 47; in metropolitan areas, 44, 46
Shifting: backward, 53; *defined*, 52; forward, 53; of burden of public debt, 110-111
Shultz, William J., *American Public Finance*, 116
Simons, Henry C., *Personal Income Taxation*, 55, 116
Size of government, 3-8, 19
Smith, Adam: on ability-to-pay principle, 55; on budget balancing, 96; on proportional taxation, 56; on scope of government, 10
Smith, Dan T., *Federal Tax Reform*, 116
Smith, W. L., *Debt Management in the United States*, 116
Smithies, Arthur, *The Budgetary Process in the United States*, 116
Social security, 22
Socialist approach to scope of government, 10, 15-16
Space exploration: collective goods, 11; expenditures, 5
Special assessments, 55
Staff Report on Employment, Growth and Price Levels, 116
Standard deduction, 59, 61
Stand-by authority, to change tax rates, 103
State and local governments, 2; advantages, 34-36; expenditures, 5-8, 37-38; growth of, 34, 42; inefficiency, 37; revenues, 37-38; tax systems, 37-38, 40-41
Stock options, 63, 75
Suburbs, economic problems of, 46, 47, 50
Supply of effort: effects of taxation, 73-75
Supply of investible funds: effects of taxation, 93
Taxation (*see also* Names of particular taxes): as source of national strength, 82; administrative qualities, 53-54; and efficiency of economy, 71-75; and growth of economy, 75-79; bases, 52; criteria of equity, 54-57; double taxation, 67-68; effects on demand, 86-87, 103; growth of revenues, 4, 37-38; issues of fairness, 61-67; multiplier effects, 86-87, 92; principles, 52-57; progressive, proportional, regressive, *defined*, 56-57, 69; rates, 40-41, 57, 75; shifting and incidence, 52; tax changes and effective demand, 85-95; temporary *vs.* permanent changes, 92, 103; variable rates, 102-103

Tax avoidance, 74-75
Tax bases, 52, 55-56; consumption, 56; income, 55; wealth, 56; other, 56
Tax credits, 60n, 62
Tax-exempt securities, 65, 75, 80
Tax Foundation Inc., *Allocation of the Income Tax Burden by Income Class*, 57
Tax havens, 46
Tax rates, 52; changes against recession and inflation, 100-102; variable, 102, 104 (*see also* Names of taxes)
Tax Revision Compendium, 116
Tax sharing, 39
Tax shelters, 64-65; life insurance, 65; pension plans, 64
Tennessee Valley Authority, 14, 16
Thompson, L. E., *Effects of Taxation on Investment by Individuals*, 79-80, 116
Time lags, in fiscal policy, 93-94, 104
Tobacco taxes, by state, 40-41
Toronto, Canada, 48
Transfer payments: expenditures, 7-8; exclusions under income tax, 58, 61; multiplier effects, 91, 103
Treasury, 21, 113
Trust funds, 22; holders of government bonds, 112n
Trusts, 75

Unemployment (*see* Full employment)
Unemployment insurance: automatic stabilizer, 89, 98; proposals to improve, 102, 104; trust fund, 22
Urban problems, 44, 45, 49
Urban renewal, 49-50; federal aid, 50

Value-added tax, 80-81, 83
Vertical equity, 55, 69
Veterans benefits, 5
Voluntary compliance system, 52, 69

Wagner, Adolph, "Wagner's Law," 8
Water resources, decision-making, 28
Water supply: economies of scale, 47; in metropolitan areas, 46
Ways and Means Committee, 21
Western Electric, 12
Wilde, Frazer B., 116
Wiseman, Jack, *The Growth of Public Expenditure in the United Kingdom*, 8-9

Yugoslavia, 15